STARTING A BUSINESS FOR BEGINNERS:

Foundations of Entrepreneurship: A Step-by-Step Guide for Aspiring Entrepreneurs.

By

Kate W. Cavill

STARTING A BUSINESS FOR BEGINNERS

Copyright

Disclaimer

STARTING A BUSINESS FOR BEGINNERS

About the author

Kate W. Cavill, the thoughtful author of the article on launching a small business, puts a plethora of expertise and helpful advice front and centre. Her thorough summary of the most important things to think about when starting a business demonstrates her knowledge.

Kate W. Cavill focus on conducting market research, spotting lucrative prospects, and matching abilities with passions shows that she takes a well-rounded and strategic approach to business growth. They successfully mentor would-be business owners on how to choose a workable business concept, carry out in-depth market research, and use their advantages to outmanoeuvre rivals.

A broad readership may easily understand the facts Kate W. Cavill writes in an engrossing and simple manner. Her use of case studies and examples to support her arguments gives readers specific advice with practical implications. Anyone thinking about starting their own business will find Kate W. Cavill's writing is motivational and motivating because of her obvious passion for the subject.

All things considered, Kate W. Cavill's writing demonstrates her knowledge and enthusiasm for supporting aspiring business owners, making it an invaluable tool for everyone attempting to negotiate the world of small business endeavours. Their advice and insights enable readers to make wise choices and build a strong basis for their success as entrepreneurs.

TABLE OF CONTENT

INTRODUCTION

In the unique universe of business, achievement isn't just about arriving at the zenith of monetary accomplishments; it's tied in with making a tradition of development and effect that reaches out past the domain of benefits. Building a manageable and flourishing business requires a comprehensive methodology that envelops monetary discernment, vital authority, and a pledge to having a constructive outcome on the planet.

By embracing development, cultivating a culture of cooperation, enabling representatives, and focusing on manageability, business visionaries can make organisations that produce abundance as well as add to a superior future. Their processes act as guides of motivation for yearning pioneers, exhibiting the force of human resourcefulness to change thoughts into the real world and make enduring effects on the world we live in.

This article will investigate the key rules that support fabricating a reasonable and flourishing business, featuring the techniques and practices that can direct hopeful business people and laid out organisations the same towards making progress in the consistently developing business scene.

We will dig into the significance of advancement and consistent improvement, investigating the force of embracing new innovations, taking on inventive methodologies, and gaining from difficulties. We will likewise analyse the urgent job of maintainability in business, stressing the need to limit natural effect, embrace feasible practices, and coordinate manageability into the plan of action and dynamic cycles.

Moreover, we will investigate the meaning of cultivating a culture of joint effort, featuring the advantages of open correspondence, shared proprietorship, cross-utilitarian cooperation, and consistent learning and improvement. By establishing a climate where various viewpoints are esteemed and utilised, organisations can open development, improve direction, and accomplish shared objectives.

The strengthening of representatives is one more foundation of a practical and flourishing business. We will examine the significance of making a work environment that values representative commitment and strengthening, putting resources into representative preparation and improvement, empowering consistent learning and development among workers, and perceiving and remunerating their commitments.

At long last, we will investigate the basic job of focusing on consumer loyalty and building solid associations with accomplices. By zeroing in on client needs and surpassing assumptions, organisations can develop reliability and reinforce their market position. Additionally, joint effort with accomplices can cultivate advancement, grow market reach, and make shared esteem.

By getting it and executing these standards, organisations can set out on an excursion towards supportability, development, and effect, leaving a positive heritage that reaches out past monetary achievement.

Chapter 1

Embark on the Exciting journey of Entrepreneurship: Your Guide to Business Success

With the prospect of enthusiasm, independence, and the ability to have a great influence, the world of entrepreneurship beckons. There's no denying the appeal of seeing ideas become reality for a lot of would-be entrepreneurs. But obstacles and uncertainty are frequently present on the road to business success.

This in-depth manual aims to provide you the necessary skills and information to successfully traverse the thrilling but challenging realm of company ownership. We will explore the essential actions you must do, such as creating an effective business strategy, obtaining capital, and building a solid web presence.

Along the road, you'll learn the fundamentals of business success—customer-centricity, flexibility, and unrelenting determination—that support company success. Don't forget that creating a successful business requires constant learning, development, and resilience.

Put on your seatbelts, fellow company owners, and get ready for an exciting journey into the world of successful operations. Let's investigate the nuances of becoming an entrepreneur, discover the keys to realising your greatest potential, and turn your ideas into attainable goals.

Unveiling the Secret to Entrepreneurial Success

Millions of individuals all over the world have been captivated and inspired by the world of business. Motivated by ingenuity, imagination, and unwavering resolve.

Crucial Elements of Successful Entrepreneurship

1. **Resilience and Adaptability:** The capacity to overcome adversity and adjust to change is one of the most important characteristics possessed by prosperous business people. They see failure as a necessary component of the business path and turn it into an opportunity to learn and develop.

2. **Drive and Enthusiasm:** Entrepreneurs that are successful do so because they have a strong drive to achieve along with a strong enthusiasm for what they do. They are able to maintain their motivation and dedication to their objectives in the face of obstacles because of their excitement.

3. **Vision and Long-Term Planning:** Establishing long-term objectives and having a clear business vision are critical for success. Entrepreneurs that are successful are able to perceive the wider picture, predict emerging trends, and make strategic plans to accomplish their goals.

4. **Networking and Relationship Building:** Prosperous business people understand the value of cultivating relationships with partners, customers, workers, and mentors as well as establishing a solid professional network.

5. **Constant Learning and Personal Growth:** Successful business people make a commitment to constant learning and personal development in order to stay ahead of the competition. They welcome the chance to learn new things and are receptive to expanding their knowledge and abilities.

Success Factors for Entrepreneurs

A variety of tactics are used by prosperous businesspeople to accomplish their objectives and keep a competitive advantage in the marketplace. Effective time management, embracing innovation, powerful branding and marketing, prudent financial management, and assembling a skilled staff are a few of these tactics.

Through the implementation of these tactics, business owners may maximise output, set themselves apart from rivals, build a strong financial base, and cultivate a positive workplace culture. The total success of their company is greatly influenced by the combination of these techniques.

1. **Effective Time Management:** Successful business people are adept at organising their schedules and recognize the importance of time. In order to maximise productivity, they assign

responsibilities, set reasonable deadlines, and prioritise activities.

2. Embracing Innovation: Entrepreneurs that are successful are always looking for new and creative methods to set themselves apart from the competition. To keep ahead of the competition, they don't mind taking measured chances and investigating novel concepts.

3. Effective Branding and Marketing: For entrepreneurs to be successful, they must build a strong brand identity and promote their goods and services efficiently. They put a lot of effort and money into developing marketing efforts that appeal to their target market.

4. Sound Financial Management: A key element of a business success story is prudent financial management. In order to secure long-term financial stability, successful entrepreneurs have a good understanding of their financial status and budget, forecast, and make data-driven decisions.

5. Creating a Talented Team: Successful business people frequently attribute their success to surrounding themselves with a talented and committed team. They recognize the value of selecting the best candidates, developing their abilities, and creating a happy workplace.

Top Entrepreneurs' Lessons

1. See Failure as a Learning Opportunity: Aspiring business owners can increase their resilience and flexibility by acknowledging that failure is a necessary part of the journey and use it as a teaching tool.

2. Find Your Passion and Follow It Unwaveringly: Finding your passion and following it with unyielding dedication will keep you inspired and dedicated to your objectives.

3. Create a Long-Term Vision and Strategy: Aspiring business owners can maintain focus by establishing specific long-term objectives and coming up with a calculated plan to meet them.

4. Develop a Strong Network: Creating and maintaining a strong professional network can lead to new prospects and growth-oriented resources.

5. Make a commitment to Personal Development and Ongoing Education: Adopting a growth mindset and continuing education will assist ambitious business owners in staying competitive in the quick-paced business world.

Charting Your Path to Entrepreneurial Success

Unquestionably, the freedom to choose your own path, the excitement of creativity, and the fulfilment of doing something meaningful make entrepreneurship alluring. But there are obstacles in the way of achieving success as an entrepreneur. It requires tenacity, perseverance, and a readiness to take lessons from both achievements and setbacks.

1. **Find Your Passion:** A strong passion is the foundation of any successful business. Even in difficult times, it serves as your motivating factor and keeps you moving forward. Choose your fire and use it as your compass, whether it's solving a difficult problem, creating something beautiful, or changing the world.

2. **Develop Your Problem-Solving Ability:** At their foundation, entrepreneurs are problem solvers. They're always looking for new and creative methods to make things better and address unmet needs. Gain experience in scenario analysis, root cause analysis, and creative problem solving.

3. **Develop a Visionary Mindset:** Successful business people are dreamers as much as doers. They have a distinct idea of the influence they hope

to have and what they hope to accomplish. Create a clear vision for yourself, put it in writing, and keep it in plain sight to help you stay motivated.

4. **Adopt a lifetime Learning Attitude:** Successful entrepreneurs are lifetime learners since the world is ever changing. Keep abreast with market developments, investigate novel technology, and never stop learning new things.

5. **Form a Robust Team:** No business person is successful on their own. Be in the company of gifted people who are passionate and share your goal.

6. **Develop Financial Discipline:** Long-term success is based on a collaborative atmosphere where ideas are openly shared, contributions are respected, and diversity is encouraged. Make wise investment selections, have a solid financial strategy, and comprehend the financial facets of your company.

7. **Put the needs of the customer first:** Clients are the lifeblood of every company. Pay attention to their input, pinpoint their unfulfilled requirements, and work to provide goods or services that genuinely improve their quality of life.

8. **See Failure as an Opportunity:** When starting a business, failures are unavoidable. However, refuse to let them define you. Consider failures as teaching opportunities, reflect on your errors, and use what you've learned to future decision-making.

9. **Develop a Growth Mindset:** Have faith in your capacity to develop and get better. Accept obstacles as chances to improve your abilities and knowledge.

10. **Never Give Up:** Starting a business has its ups and downs. You'll have moments when you want to give up. But never forget where you came from, and never give up on your goals.

Chapter 2

Laying the foundation for sucess: crafting a compelling business plan

A well-written business plan serves as a road map for your venture's success in the fast-paced entrepreneurial environment of today. A thorough business plan is essential for any kind of entrepreneur, from seasoned business owners to aspiring startup founders. It is the means by which you may obtain capital, make wise choices, and successfully negotiate the always changing economic landscape.

A well-crafted business plan forms the basis of a successful endeavour, coordinating with essential components like the Business Model Canvas and adjusting to the dynamic business landscape. Since we at Digital Leadership recognize the value of these strategic underpinnings, we provide organisations with full services in Digital Strategy Consulting and Business Model Strategy to help them not only survive but prosper in the current competitive environment.

What is a business plan?

A written document known as a business plan contains a company's objectives, strategies, and comprehensive financial and operational plans. It acts as a road plan for the company, giving its expansion and development a defined course. The purpose and vision of the firm, its goods and services, market analysis, competitors, target market, marketing and sales tactics, organisational structure, financial forecasts, and finance requirements are all often included in a business plan. Business plans are frequently used to direct a company's operations, get capital from lenders or investors, and explain the company's goals and strategy to stakeholders.

Typically, a traditional company strategy is divided into two main sections:

- The Explaining Section:

Written material that aims to give a thorough overview of the firm and/or the business concept is included in this section. It includes sections like the executive summary, business overview, market analysis, specifics of the product or service, sales and marketing plans, organisational structure, operational designs, and financial requirements.

- The Section on Finance:

This part contains financial estimates and statistics, including balance sheets, income statements, cash flow forecasts, and comprehensive details about sources and requirements for finance. This section provides a quantitative assessment of the company's financial status and projections for the future.

Important Elements of a Business Plan

For entrepreneurs and company executives looking to steer their companies toward success, creating a comprehensive and engaging business plan is a critical first step. A well-organised business plan not only acts as a growth roadmap for your company but also effectively conveys to partners, investors, and other stakeholders your vision, strategy, and potential. The essential elements of a strong business plan provide insightful analysis and useful advice to assist you in crafting a document that instils confidence and unites your team around a common goal. Every important component is essential to creating a business plan that can lead your company toward long-term success and obtain funding. Let's examine these elements in more detail so that the story in your business plan has more substance and clarity.

1. **Executive Synopsis:** The main points of your company strategy should be briefly summarised in this part. The market potential, your distinct value offer, revenue forecasts, financial needs, and the overall objectives of the company should all be briefly discussed.

2. **Description of the Company:** Give a detailed account of your company's past, highlighting noteworthy events and accomplishments. Establish your purpose, vision, and values clearly so that everyone can understand what motivates the company's actions and culture.

3. **Examination of the Market:** Examine the market's subtleties by talking about its size, growth rate, dynamics, and trends. Emphasise the particular client profiles, target market segments, and pain problems that your company seeks to solve. Provide a SWOT

(Strengths, Weaknesses, Opportunities, and Threats) analysis to demonstrate your grasp of the market environment.

4. **Goods or Services:** Provide a thorough description of your offerings, highlighting their salient characteristics and advantages. Explain how these services address particular client demands or issues, and provide an explanation of any intellectual property or proprietary technologies.

5. **Sales & Marketing Plan:** Give a thorough synopsis of your sales and marketing strategies. Go into great detail about your price plan and how it fits the characteristics of the market. Describe your marketing strategies, both traditional and digital ones, and your distribution channels.

6. **Structure of Organization:** Provide a brief biography of each important team member, highlighting their responsibilities within the

company and their relevant experience and skills. Provide an organisational chart to show the reporting lines and expandability of the structure.

7. **Operational Plan:** Describe your everyday activities in great detail, including facility needs, technology use, supply chain management, and manufacturing procedures. Talk about scaling techniques and quality control procedures.

8. **Financial Projections:** For a minimum of three to five years, provide a comprehensive breakdown of financial estimates, including monthly or quarterly projections. Describe the underlying assumptions of these figures, taking into account things like pricing policies and market growth rates. Emphasise important financial measures such as return on investment, client acquisition expenses, and burn rate.

9. **Required Funding:** Indicate precisely how much money you're looking for, why you need the money, and how you plan to use it to reach your goals. Describe possible financial options, including grants, loans, and equity investments. Make the anticipated terms and conditions clear.

10. **Addendum:** Provide other information in the appendix that further bolster the depth and legitimacy of your business plan. Market research papers, letters of intent, patents, contracts, prototypes, and any other pertinent documents that strengthen your case might be included in this.

The essence of a Business Plan: A Roadmap to Success

An effective business plan is a crucial tool for entrepreneurs, small company owners, and their staff members as it allows them to set objectives and monitor their success as their enterprise expands. When launching a new company, the first task should be business planning. In order to attract investors and help them decide whether your firm is worthwhile, business plans are also crucial. Generally, a business plan contains comprehensive details that might raise the likelihood of success for your enterprise, such as:

- Performing a market study entails learning about the variables and circumstances influencing your sector.
- Analysing your rivals' strengths and shortcomings is known as competitive analysis.
- Customer segmentation: to enhance your marketing, split your clientele up into various groups according to particular attributes.
- Marketing: promoting your company through the use of your research

- Plans for logistics and operations: organising and carrying out the most productive manufacturing process
- Being aware of how much money comes into and goes out of your organisation through cash flow prediction "a comprehensive route to sustained growth".

Ten Justifications for having a Business Strategy

I can read your mind: "Do I truly require a showcasing procedure? In addition to the fact that they seem out of date, it sounds like a lot of effort, and I like to figure things out as I go.

The short answer is that a business strategy is indeed necessary! "Starting one more business without a philosophy seems to be going on a mountain adventure without a helper or GPS support — you'll ultimately get lost and starve!" observed businessman Kevin J. Donaldson. firm plans are essential to beginning a firm and positioning yourself for success, despite the fact that they may seem laborious and time-consuming.

1. **To assist you in making important decisions:** A business plan's main value lies in its ability to facilitate improved decision-making. Being an entrepreneur is frequently a never-ending game of crisis management and decision making. It's not always possible for small firms to take the time to sit down and carefully weigh all the possible outcomes of a particular choice. An organisation procedure can assist with that.

You may find the answers to some of the most important business choices in advance by creating a company plan.

Writing a strong business plan is a necessary evil that forces you to sit down and consider important aspects of your venture before you launch, such as your product line and marketing approach. A lot of difficult questions are answered by you in advance. Additionally, giving your primary methods a lot of thought may assist you in comprehending how those choices will affect your overall approach.

2. **To work out the kinks:** Creating a business plan necessitates that entrepreneurs pose many difficult questions to themselves and take the time to develop thoughtful, in-depth responses. Writing a paper can help you express your vision in more concrete terms and identify any holes in your plan, even if the document itself vanishes as soon as it's finished.

3. **To steer clear of the major error in company plans:** CB Insights analysis indicates that the following are some of the most typical causes of company failure:

- **No Market Need:** Your product is not wanted by anyone.

- **Lack of Capital:** Problems with cash flow or plain out of company cash.
- **Insufficient Team:** This emphasises how crucial it is to appoint the best candidates to assist you in managing your company.
- **Stiff Competition**: When there are a lot of rivals in your industry, it might be difficult to turn a consistent profit.
- **Pricing:** Some business owners set their prices for their goods or services excessively high or too low, which can both lead to unhappiness.

Making a company strategy is an exercise that might assist you in avoiding these significant errors. Every section of a business plan, including cash flow estimates and product-market fit analyses, can assist in identifying some of those potentially serious errors before they happen. For instance, if it turns out there is no market demand, don't be scared to abandon a truly great concept. Tell the truth to yourself!

4. **To Demonstrate the Business's Viability**: While enthusiasm may be a powerful motivator, it's not a very good way to demonstrate a business's viability. Developing a detailed plan for transforming your idea into a profitable company is maybe the most crucial stage between concept and execution. You may verify that your brilliant concept makes good commercial sense with the aid of business planning.

The statistical surveying component of your business procedure is fundamental. Market research may provide in-depth understanding of your target market, rivals, and sector of business. It may help entrepreneurs who are launching a new company as well as current companies by providing them with improved knowledge on marketing, advertising, and the introduction of new goods and services.

5. **To Establish more Appropriate Benchmarks and Objectives:** In the absence of a company strategy, goals tend to become arbitrary and lack direction. The purpose and significance of such benchmarks may be increased with the use of a company strategy. They can also provide you with insights into how your plan is (or isn't) coming together over time and help you stay accountable to your long-term vision and strategy.

6. **To Convey Goals and Expectations**: You can't always be the one to make all of the decisions, whether you're leading a team of two or one hundred people. Consider the business plan as an acting instructor, available to respond to inquiries whenever there is a lapse in instruction. Inform your employees that if they have any questions or are unable to receive a response from you immediately, they can always go to the company plan to find out what to do next.

Sharing your company strategy with your team members also makes it more likely that everyone will grasp your long-term goals and be in agreement with what you're doing and why.

7. **To Offer Guidance to Service Providers:** In order to assist them with responsibilities like accounting, marketing, legal support, and consulting, small companies usually hire contractors, freelancers, and other specialists. A well-crafted business plan guarantees that all stakeholders are in agreement and facilitates the sharing of pertinent portions with those who are essential to the organisation's success.

8. **To Obtain Funding:** Did you know that having a business plan increases your chances of funding by 2.5 times? A business plan is probably required if you intend to borrow money from a bank, pitch to venture capitalists, or think about selling your firm in the future. Ultimately, potential investors will

want to know that their money is well-managed and that the business will remain sustainable. The best ways to demonstrate it are through business plans, which are normally necessary for anybody looking for outside funding.

9. **To Gain a Deeper Comprehension of the Overall Environment:** No company is an island, and even if you may be well-versed in everything that goes on within your walls, it's crucial to comprehend the competitive environment as well. You may gain a deeper understanding of your competitors and the larger industry by creating a business plan. It can also help you identify possible disruptions, customer trends and preferences, and other insights that aren't necessarily immediately apparent.

10. **To Lower Risk**: Although starting a business is a hazardous endeavour, the risk is much easier to handle when it is put to the test by a well-written

business plan. Creating operational and logistical planning, analysing the market and competitive environment, and projecting income and expenses may all help lower the risk associated with an inherently unstable source of income. You may take smarter decisions, leave less to chance, and have the clearest picture of your company's future with a business plan.

Defining Your Business Concept: Identifying Your Niche and Target Audience

The most crucial stage in launching a company is defining your idea. Choosing your target market and specialty is part of this.

A Niche: what is it?

A niche refers to a particular area within a market. It is a collection of individuals with similar needs or interests. Women who are interested in large bags, for instance, might represent a niche market for bags.

Why is determining your specialty so important?

Finding your niche enables you to concentrate your marketing and sales efforts on a certain demographic. This can assist you in more successfully and efficiently reaching your target audience.

How to find your specialty

There are several methods for determining your specialty. Considering your own abilities and interests is one method. Regarding what do you have a strong passion for? What are your areas of expertise? After determining your interests and abilities, you may begin to consider how you might use them to benefit a certain population.

Another method for determining your specialty is to examine the market. What diverse requirements and interests do the individuals in your target market have? What are the current market trends? Finding a market niche in which to compete might be your first step in developing a solid grasp of the industry.

A Target Audience: what is it?

The particular set of people you wish to market your goods or services to is known as your target audience. It is crucial to take into account the demands, psychographics, and demographics of your target audience while identifying them.

- **Characteristics:**

The measurable traits of a population, such as age, gender, income, and education level, are known as its demographics. The demographics of the individuals you wish to contact should be taken into account when determining your target audience.

- **Psychometric data**:

The intangible traits of a population, such as values, interests, and lifestyles, are known as psychographics. The psychographic traits of the individuals you wish to contact should be taken into account when establishing your target audience.

It's critical to take the requirements of the individuals you wish to reach into account when establishing your target audience. What hurts them the most? Which issues are they attempting to resolve? You may create goods or services that satisfy your target audience's wants if you are aware of what they are.

The most effective method to Figure out Who Your Objective Market Is:

Examine your current clientele: Which clients are the most profitable for you? What are their requirements, psychographics, and demographics?

You may begin to find new people that are similar to your current clients after you have a solid grasp of them.

Examine your rivals: Who are the people your rivals are aiming for? Which marketing messages do they use? You can begin to find other customers that your rivals aren't serving after you have a solid grasp of them.

You may begin developing your company concept once you have determined your target market and specialisation. This entails outlining your value proposition, marketing plan, and goods or services.

You may improve your chances of succeeding in the business world by precisely identifying your target market and specialisation.

Evaluating the Viability of the Market: In order to evaluate the market viability and ascertain whether your niche has the capacity to last, you must examine market trends, rivalry, and economic variables. You can decide whether your company is successful by being knowledgeable about the present situation of the market. Start by looking at market trends to find any changes or new possibilities that might affect your specialty.

Next, evaluate how many competitors there are in the industry and what makes you stand out from them by analysing the competitive landscape. Take into account other economic aspects that may have an impact on the demand for your goods or services, such as consumer spending patterns and general market circumstances.

You may determine whether there is a market for your niche and whether it is worthwhile to pursue by carefully analysing these components.

Articulating your Mission and Vision: Setting the Direction for your Venture.

Sometimes, entrepreneurs are likened to superheroes: They find solutions to issues. They have a lot of authority and duty. In the same manner that superheroes take on enemies, they are risk-takers. In the face of failure, they remain unfazed. In order to provide solutions that go beyond meeting each customer's specific needs, they continuously enhance their goods and look for answers. Individuals frequently comment, "If by some stroke of good luck I'd thought about that!" after an entrepreneur achieves success.

Still, thinking is insufficient. Moreover, doing is insufficient. Entrepreneurs who are successful also know how important it is to explain the history and purpose of their business. In addition to finding solutions, they also share tales of triumphs over enemies, near-miss disasters, and agonising losses that taught them how to start over. What good is a hero, after all, if not for his or her backstory, legends, and victories in conflicts and markets?

These origin myths are considered sacrosanct in superhero stories. A problem-solution narrative is similar to the origin tale of an offering for an entrepreneur. The problem-solution story succinctly outlines a particular issue that impacts a large number of people and positions the good or service as an original, thoughtful, and creative answer.

More is required to maintain focus during a string of successes and setbacks than just a problem-solution story: A mission statement, goals, and a vision are all necessary. These were covered in The Entrepreneurial Perspective, but as you work on your story and hone your pitch to employers, investors, and consumers, you should review them. A formal presentation where you make a request is called a pitch. It is (often) given to prospective startup investors.

VISION

As you learned in The Entrepreneurial Perspective, a vision statement describes the company's overarching goal and what the entrepreneur envisions the endeavour developing into in the future. You need to develop a vision statement that enables you to look into the future and answer the question, "What might we become someday if our organisation were the best possible version of itself?" before you can make an engaged statement of purpose and objectives that address what your identity is, what you do, and what you intend to do from here on out.

The process of creating a vision statement involves ideation, which is the deliberate process of allowing one's mind to wander from a stated goal or problem in a variety of directions. In this case, the goal is to generate new possibilities for products, services, or procedures that will help your venture succeed. Compared to a mission statement, a vision statement is more flexible.

Examine your organisation's industry as a whole to develop a compelling vision statement. Be broad. Describe a dream that, while not yet achievable, captures the best-case scenario for your group's results. Creating a vision statement helps your organisation as a whole identify important areas for potential growth and important social influences you can have. However, as a general rule, you should keep an eye out for changes in your industry or sector and revisit your vision when those may call for a change. For instance, Netflix began by renting out DVDs with the intention of giving consumers the best possible value and convenience. However, it had to adapt when platforms for consuming entertainment developed, and it now specialises in television streaming content. The company's mission statement for 2019 is "Building the greatest worldwide entertainment distribution network."

Write queries like "How might we..." or statements like "In a perfect world, our organisation would..." while creating your vision statement. Create a vision statement that centres around the organisation's service objectives and transforms it into a sustainable social benefit. (Instead of promising to bring about global peace or give everyone a pet, you could observe how companies in your industry run and aspire to perform more socially and strategically.)

These actions offer a suitable place to start:

- Describe how, in an ideal world, your organisation would operate.

- Link the aspirations of your company to more general aspirations for advancement.
- Describe how your goods and services will contribute to improving the world in the future.

It's not necessary for dreams to be outrageous to be popular or significant. The organisation's vision statement aims to foster an environment of free communication rather than impose unrealistic expectations. A vision statement that is devoid of any solid foundation is easily dismissed; similarly, if it emphasises goals like market share and product development—that is, goals that are concrete and mission-oriented—it misses the mark. Let your best team perform to the best of its abilities using future affordances and capacities made available by other creators and entrepreneurs like you. Then, articulate the potential impact that you could have as world changers. Once more, the intention is not to create unrealistic expectations or require unceasing innovation from contributors and those who work in positions that support daily operations. The idea is to start a discussion about the possibilities for the company. Smaller beginning businesses (like delis or coffee shops, for instance) may have a more straightforward goal, but it will still be centred on giving customers a special experience. Put otherwise, it ought to remain aspirational and connected to the goal statement.

Samples of Vision Statements

IKEA's	To improve everyone's quality of life on a daily basis
Alzheimer's Association	An Alzheimer's disease-free world

Parker Warby	To set the standard for socially responsible businesses and provide designer eyewear at a cutting-edge pricing.

A vision statement can be powerful even if it is short. Just fifteen words make up one well-known vision statement: "At IKEA, our vision is to create a better everyday life for the many people." This vision statement highlights IKEA's goals and what its employees should strive to become: people who improve other people's quality of life on a daily basis. Take note of the word "the many people." This is intentional: IKEA chooses to match its vision with the large number of individuals who are its target market while producing mass-marketed goods. This vision statement outlines a wide, good conclusion and is not intended to be interpreted as a political declaration. Rather, it is an ideal set for the global brand. In a way, IKEA's statement is pure vision. Rather than attempting to sketch an implementation plan, a vision statement should relate the daily activities of a company to a common ideal.

Having said that, the corporation also presents its "business idea" in addition to its vision. "To offer an extensive variety of very much planned, practical home outfitting items at costs so low that whatever number individuals as would be prudent will actually want to bear the cost of them" is the secret our business idea is expressed. This can be thought of as both a mission statement and a value proposition combined. A value proposition, which is a key component of any pitch, describes precisely what a company or organisation offers that customers will pay for (or donate to, in the case of a nonprofit). Value propositions are essential for spotting possibilities, as we discovered in Finding

Entrepreneurial possibilities. In Business Model and Plan, you will discover how they fit into your business plan. However, the topic of this chapter's discussion is how and why it's necessary to communicate the value proposition.

Mision

An organisation's or business's purpose is its entrepreneurial mission. It contains a sense of action and is articulated as a self-conceptualization within a marketplace. Relevant questions to think about while evaluating a venture's mission include: Who are we? How do we create or act? What is the initial reason for our being as a business? The goal of Apple co-founders Steve Jobs and Steve Wozniak was to make personal computers accessible to common people, which required them to develop basic software (such as a mouse and graphical user interface) along with hardware.

An organisation's identity and goals are established by a well-developed sense of mission. There are charitable organisations in markets as well. They must fight for resources and establish their identity through the services they offer. Having a well-defined mission is beneficial when a nonprofit is looking for funding. It assists business owners in the for-profit sector in justifying their "thing," whatever it may be, to consumers, employees, and investors.

One of the oldest and most well-known relief organisations in the country, the American Red Cross, for instance, has a very clear mission statement: "The American Red Cross mobilises the power of volunteers and the generosity of donors to prevent and alleviate human suffering in the face of emergencies." Success in an organisation depends on having a well-defined mission statement.

A mission statement articulates the main objective of an organisation and serves as a concise plan of action to achieve it. It is a concise description of the company's purpose. In order to write a mission statement, respond to these inquiries:

We are who we are.

How do we create or act?

What is the purpose of our enterprise?

Creating and upholding a successful mission statement not only demonstrates to prospective partners and customers that your organisation knows where it is headed, but it also brings people of the organisation together. Although mission statements can be amended, it is preferable to start with a proper one. A compelling mission statement should direct decisions and assist stakeholders in prioritising the entity's next actions.

Clarity is essential when creating a mission statement that works: It needs to be precise. A mission statement's omissions might be just as significant as its inclusions. A strong mission statement is clear, concise, and truthful about the organisation's strengths as well as the relevant market. It finds the ideal ratio between hope and pragmatism.

"At Toys Inc., we make the highest quality wooden toys available anywhere, and our central goal is to keep on developing to be a market chief in the exemplary toy industry" could be the wording of an insufficient mission statement. This might make a stronger mission statement: "Toys Inc. is a market leader in the manufacturing of wooden toys in North America." Our goal is to become the industry leader in the production of wooden puzzles and toy cars made of wood, as well as to provide customers with new takes on vintage toys. While there is space for improvement in both mission statements, the second one provides a clearer definition of the organisation's current situation and long-term goals.

Clichés should not be used in a mission statement since they limit the venture's specific and distinctive vision. It should make reference to customers or clients and shouldn't stifle creativity or innovation.

Identifying the organisation is the first step in crafting a compelling mission statement. You already know the main issue to solve and the direction you want to take the product—and thus the brand—even as a startup. When articulating the mission of your company, be precise while preserving your opportunities for expansion. Incorporate or integrate the mission of service into the overarching goal.

Once more, the mission statement must accomplish the following goals in an upbeat manner:

Describe your identity.

Specify what you do and for whom right now.

Decide on your goals for the future.

Early on in a startup, the mission may shift significantly. A company's ability to pivot, or modify its value proposition to better achieve product-market fit, should not be restricted by the design of its mission statement (for a more thorough discussion on pivoting, go to Launch for Growth to Success). Additionally, while they shouldn't be immune to change, only make essential and beneficial revisions to the mission statement. When an organisation or company makes a significant change (because of an acquisition, a change in focus, a new growth plan, etc.), or if their purpose has changed significantly, they typically update their mission statement.

For instance, the March of Dimes organisation was established initially to assist those suffering from polio; but, due to the effectiveness of polio vaccinations, the illness was declared eradicated in the United States. Consequently, the March of Dimes shifted its objectives to include preventing infant mortality, premature birth, and birth abnormalities. As another illustration, Slack was created as a platform for online game makers to communicate. It is a venture-backed firm that went public in the middle of 2019. The initial business failed (again), but the founder saw that his engineers were collaborating quickly with each other and didn't require email or other Windows features. This shift was swiftly announced by Slack in a straightforward mission statement: "Slack is where workflows are." It's the place where you can collaborate with the people you need, share information, and get the tools you need to complete tasks.

It is important to remember that improving mission and vision statements is not an organisation's goal. An organisation's goal is to benefit people while attempting to gain funding or other support in the process. Creating mission and vision statements is done to help you achieve that. Your mission statement serves as your approach in the real world of business, while your vision statement essentially expresses your dream. The mission statement focuses on the potential beneficiaries of the venture, whereas the vision statement highlights the significance of the organisation and its future trajectory. Refining these assertions will assist you with explaining your innovative story. Clarifying your entrepreneurial story will be aided by honing these statements.

Conducting Market Analysis: Understand your Competitors and Industry Landscape

A comprehensive evaluation of a market within a particular industry is known as a market analysis. There are numerous advantages to these evaluations, including lower company risk and improved decision-making. Although conducting a market analysis on your own can take a lot of time, it is simple and quick to do.

Use the procedures in this guide to conduct a market analysis for your company.

What is included in a market analysis?

You will examine your market's dynamics in a market analysis, including volume and value, prospective client segments, purchasing trends, rivalry, and other crucial elements. The following queries should be addressed in a comprehensive marketing analysis:

- **Who might be my potential clients?**
- **What purchasing patterns do my customers have?**
- **What size market is my aim for?**
- **What price range do buyers have for my product?**
- **Who are my primary rivals?**
- **What are the advantages and disadvantages of my rivals?**
- **What are the advantages of doing a study on marketing?**

A marketing analysis can assist estimate income, lower risk, and spot new trends. A marketing analysis can be used during various phases of your company's development, and it may even be advantageous to carry out one annually to stay abreast of any significant shifts in the industry.

Your business plan will often include a thorough market analysis since it will help you better understand your target market and competitors. This will assist you in developing a marketing plan that is more focused.

Performing a market analysis has the following significant advantages:

1. **Mitigation of risk:** Understanding your market will help you make better business decisions since you'll be aware of the key players in your sector, significant market trends, and what it takes to succeed. You can also perform a SWOT analysis, which highlights your company's strengths, weaknesses, opportunities, and threats, to assist you better safeguard your enterprise.

2. **Products or services that are specifically targeted:** When you know exactly what your customers want from you, you can serve them much more effectively. Knowing who your consumers are

will help you better cater your business's offerings to meet their needs.

3. **Emerging trends:** Being the first to recognize a new opportunity or trend is frequently key to staying ahead in business. Staying abreast of industry trends through marketing analysis is a wonderful method to position yourself to capitalise on this knowledge.

4. **Revenue forecasts:** Since it projects the numbers, traits, and trends of your target market into the future, a market forecast is a crucial part of most marketing analyses. This lets you know what kind of profits to anticipate, so you can modify your budget and company plan appropriately.

5. **Evaluation benchmarks:** Measuring the success of your company beyond just the metrics can be challenging. Key performance indicators (KPIs) or benchmarks are provided by a market analysis,

allowing you to assess your business and compare it to others in your industry.

6. **Context for previous errors:** Marketing analytics can clarify previous errors made by your company or unusualities in the sector. Comprehensive analytics, for instance, can clarify the factors that affected a particular product's sales or the reasons behind a metric's performance. Because you'll be able to identify and explain what went wrong and why, this can assist you prevent repeating those errors or encountering similar anomalies.

7. **Marketing optimization:** Here's where an annual marketing analysis comes in helpful. A frequent analysis may help you identify the areas of your marketing that need improvement and those that are functioning well when compared to other businesses in your industry. It can also provide guidance for your ongoing marketing efforts.

Your company may gain a lot from market research, particularly if you perform them frequently to ensure that your marketing campaigns are informed with the most recent data.

How to carry out a market study

Even though performing a marketing study is not a difficult process, it does require extensive, focused research, so allow enough time to complete the task.

The seven steps involved in performing a market analysis are as follows:

1. Establish your goal: There are a variety of reasons to perform a market analysis, including understanding a new market or assessing your competitors. Whatever your motivation, it's critical to establish it early on in order to stay on course. First, determine if your goal is external, such as obtaining a business loan, or internal, such as enhancing your cash flow or business operations.

Your goal will determine the kind and volume of research you conduct.

2. Examine the industry's current state:

Draw a thorough picture of your industry's current situation. Include the apparent direction of the industry using measures like size, trends, and expected growth, and provide ample evidence to back up your conclusions. To identify your competitive advantage in your particular market, you can also perform a comparative market analysis.

3. Determine who your target consumer is. You shouldn't waste your time trying to pique the interest of everyone on the planet because not everyone will be your customer. Rather, determine who is most likely to want your product by conducting a target market analysis, then concentrate your efforts there. You should be aware of the size of your market, the demographics of your clientele, their origins, and

any factors that might affect their purchasing choices. Examine the following demographic variables:

Age Gender Place of Employment

Needs for Education

Passions

As you conduct your research, you may want to think about developing a persona or customer profile that represents your ideal client to use as a template for your marketing campaigns.

4. Recognize your rivals: In order to succeed, you must have a thorough awareness of your rivals' advantages, disadvantages, and market saturation as well as what sets them apart from you. Make a list of all of your primary rivals first, then proceed to analyse each one using the SWOT method. What is it that the company has that you don't? Why would a

consumer pick that company over yours? Consider yourself as the client.

Next, order your list of rivals by degree of hazard, and select a deadline for performing recurring SWOT evaluations on your most dangerous rivals.

5. Compile further information:

You can never have too much data while doing marketing analysis, therefore information is your friend. It is crucial that the information you utilise is reliable and accurate, so pay attention to where you obtain your statistics. Here are a few reliable sources of business data:

- **National Center for Labor Statistics**
- **Census Bureau of the United States**
- **State and local websites for commerce**
- **Trade publications**
- **Your personal SWOT evaluations**
- **Questionnaires or market surveys**

6. evaluate your data: In order to make sense of the information you have gathered and confirmed to be accurate, you must evaluate it. Sort your research into areas that make sense for you, but make sure to include those related to your goals, your target audience, and your competitors.

The following are the key components that your study have to cover:

- An overview of the size and growth rate of your industry
- The anticipated market share percentage for your company
- A forecast for the industry
- Trends in consumer purchasing
- Your anticipated expansion
- How much buyers are prepared to spend on your good or service

7. Apply the analysis you've done: It's time to put your market analysis to use after you've generated it. Examine internally how your business can benefit from the research and conclusions you have obtained. Have you observed practices in other companies that you would like to adopt for your own? Are there techniques to increase the efficacy of your marketing campaigns?

To facilitate sharing of your study with lenders, if you perform your analysis for outside parties, arrange your data and research into a document that is simple to read and understand.

To stay on top of your market, save all of your data and research for your upcoming study. You might also want to try setting up a yearly calendar reminder.

Formulating Financial Projections: Forecasting Revenue, Expenses and Profitability

What are Financial Projections used for?

Monetary estimating fills in as a valuable device for key partners, both inside and beyond the business. They often are used for:

1. **Business planning:** Accurate financial projections can help a company establish growth targets and other goals. They're additionally used to decide if thoughts like another product offering are monetarily achievable. Future monetary evaluations are useful instruments for business possibility arranging, which includes thinking about the money related effect of unfavourable occasions and most pessimistic scenario situations. They likewise give a benchmark: In the event that income is missing the mark concerning projections, for instance, the organisation might require changes to keep business

procedure on target. Projections might uncover likely issues — say, startling working costs that surpass cash inflows. A negative income projection might recommend the business needs to get subsidising through external ventures or bank credits, increment deals, further develop edges, or cut costs.

2. **Investors:** When potential investors consider putting their money into a venture, they want a return on that investment. Business projections are a key instrument they will use to go with that choice. The projections can figure in laying out the valuation of your business, value stakes, plans for an exit, and that's just the beginning. Financial backers may likewise utilise your projections to guarantee that the business is meeting objectives and benchmarks.

3. **Advances or credit extensions:** Moneylenders depend on monetary projections to decide if to

stretch out a business credit to your organisation. They'll need to see authentic monetary information like income articulations, your asset report, and other budget summaries — however they'll likewise look carefully at your long term monetary projections. Great competitors can get higher advance sums with lower loan fees or more adaptable instalment plans.

Banks may likewise utilise the assessed worth of organisation resources to decide the insurance to get the credit. Like financial backers, banks commonly allude to your projections after some time to screen progress and monetary wellbeing.

What data is remembered for monetary projections for a business?

What is the purpose of financial projections?

Key stakeholders inside and outside the company can benefit from financial forecasting. Frequently, they are employed for:

a. Planning a business: Precise financial estimates can assist a business in setting expansion objectives and other ambitions. They are also used to assess the financial viability of concepts like new product lines. For corporate contingency planning, which takes into account the monetary impact of unfavourable occurrences and worst-case scenarios, future financial estimations are useful tools. They also offer a standard: For instance, the business may need to make adjustments if revenue isn't meeting expectations in order to maintain business operations. Projections can highlight possible issues, such as unforeseen operating costs that surpass financial inflows. A negative cash flow forecast can indicate that the company needs to raise money from bank loans or outside investments, boost sales, boost margins, or make expense reductions.

b. Traders: Potential investors seek a return on their investment before considering investing in a project. One important tool they'll need to get that conclusion is a business projection. The projections may be used to determine your company's valuation, equity stakes, exit strategy, and other factors. Your forecasts could also be used by investors to make sure the company is hitting targets and benchmarks.

c. Credit lines or loans: Financial predictions are used by lenders to decide whether to offer your organisation a business loan. They will review your multi-year financial plans closely in addition to your previous financial data, which includes cash flow statements, your balance sheet, and other financial documents. Stronger candidates may be eligible for longer loan terms, cheaper interest rates, or more accommodating repayment schedules.

The estimated worth of the company's assets may also be used by lenders to establish the collateral needed to get a loan. Lenders, like investors, usually review your estimates over time to assess your financial health and growth.

What details are included in a company's financial projections?

You must gather some information before you can begin to develop projections. Existing business owners can make use of three financial statements that they most likely already possess:

A cash flow statement; a balance sheet; an annual income statement; respectively.

Yet, a new company won't have access to this prior information. Thus, market research is essential: Examine price tactics used by rivals, go through market analyses and research papers, and carefully examine any additional publicly accessible information that can support your estimates. You can get started by starting with basic calculations and conservative estimations, and you can always add to the projections as time goes on.

Financial projections from different businesses may differ in level of detail, but they usually depend on and incorporate the following:

Money Movement

As implied by the name, a cash flow statement displays the inflow and outflow of cash for the company over time. There are three primary categories for cash flows:

1. carrying out operations: These cash flows are a result of the company's primary operations; they include revenue from sales of products and services as well as expenses for rent, taxes, and salaries.

2. Investment-related activities: This includes any transaction involving the purchase or sale of long-term assets that aren't cash equivalents, such as non-physical assets like intellectual property or patents, or physical assets like land or equipment. This covers the sale of stocks, bonds, and other securities that have been owned for a minimum of a year.

3. financing operations: Financial activity is represented by this flow, which includes taking in money through bank or investor loans, paying interest on those debts, issuing or repurchasing shares, and paying dividends.

Statement of Income

The company's revenue and expenses for a specific time are predicted in projected income statements, also called projected profit and loss statements (P&Ls).

This is typically a table where each category has multiple line items. The sales forecast for each specific good or service can be included in sales projections (many organisations divide this down by month). The arrangement for expenses is similar: Enumerate all of your anticipated costs, broken down by category. Don't forget to include variable costs for raw materials and transportation, in addition to recurrent charges like rent and salary.

A net income projection—that is, the difference between your revenue and expenses, including any taxes or interest—will also be given to you as a result of this exercise. This document is sometimes referred to as a P&L because that figure represents your projected profit or loss.

Equilibrium Report

A balance sheet provides a quick overview of the financial situation of your business at a certain moment in time. There are three significant components listed as balance sheet items:

1. Assets Any tangible thing of value that the business possesses or may acquire in the future, such as cash, inventory, equipment, and accounts receivable, is considered an asset. Copyrights, trademarks, patents, and other intellectual property are examples of intangible assets.

2. Liabilities: Taxes, salaries, dividends, accounts payable, and unearned income, such as payments from customers for things you haven't yet provided, are all examples of what the firm owes.

3. Owner Equity: The amount of shareholder equity is calculated by deducting all liabilities from all assets. It shows how much capital, or money, the company would have had left over if it paid off all of its debts at once or

went out of business (this amount may be negative if debt exceeds assets). The amount of capital invested in a firm by its owners and other shareholders is known as equity.

Because assets always equal liabilities plus shareholder equity, these are known as balance sheets.

How to create financial projections for your business in five easy stages

- Determine the goal and duration of your forecasts.
- Compile pertinent historical financial information and market research.
- Estimate your costs.
- Projected sales
- Create financial forecasts.

You may simplify the process of creating financial estimates for your business by following these five steps:

1. Determine the goal and duration of your forecasts.

Depending on why you are making them, your forecasts may include different information. Are they for long-term performance tracking, investor pitching, or internal planning? Determine the time period (monthly, quarterly, yearly, or multi-year) so that the subsequent processes may be adjusted accordingly.

2. Compile pertinent historical financial information and market research.

Collect previous financial statements, such as balance sheets, cash flow statements, and yearly income statements, if they are available. Without this historical evidence, new businesses could be forced to rely on industry standards, analyst reports, and market research—all of which established businesses should also employ to bolster their presumptions.

3. Projected costs

Based on the direct costs of manufacturing your goods and services (cost of goods sold, or COGS) and operational expenditures, which include both one-time and recurrent charges, determine your future spending. Allow for anticipated variations in costs, as they might alter with time, as a result of new product introductions, business expansion, and market experience.

4. Projected sales

Projected monthly sales for every source of income. These estimates, which might be based on previous data or market research, should take into consideration expected or future shifts in price and market demand.

5. Create budgetary estimates

Upon obtaining your anticipated costs and earnings, you can enter them into Shopify's cash flow calculator and cash flow statement template. Your income statement may be predicted using this information as well. These procedures therefore help you with your balance sheet computations, where

you will also record all of your assets and liabilities.

CHAPTER 3

Securing the Financial Backbone: Finding your Entrepreneurial Dreams

What comes to mind when you consider the components that make up your company's financial foundation? Is the group involved? The accounts of the finances? Actually, it's more than just these two taken together. The financial core of a company functions best when all the parts are turning in unison, which is one of the main drivers of performance achievement. How could you strengthen your financial foundation?

Here are three Strategies for Laying a Solid Foundation:

1. Assemble the appropriate team: "We got a handle on we planned to major areas of strength for have for a general this year... in any case, we other than

recalled that we expected to require a couple of locale front and centre, so it required a long time to sort out the specific blends and staff that we must rest on when the postseason "It all started," Brigham Youthful College Rugby's main trainer David Smyth remarked of his team during the 2014 mission. Nonetheless, I accept that when we settled it and the players had the option to comprehend their obligations, we had the option to build and play some brilliant rugby

You have the same opportunity as Coach Smyth to assess your squad, maximise your advantages, and minimise your disadvantages. In a financial team, each job has an obligation to cover tasks that the other roles cannot perform as effectively.

Occasionally, entrepreneurs cling to the notion of accomplishing the maximum amount without the need to expand their present workforce, which may ultimately cause more harm than good. Working efficiently requires aligning your financial portfolio with your growth objectives. While one eCommerce company may be just getting started with basic inventory management, another company in the same sector may be experiencing explosive growth, and growing with a small team of accountants won't be possible. A controller or CFO may be needed for the second company. You may identify your demands and choose the kind of financial specialists you need by actively evaluating your performance levels and goals.

What distinguishes the various financial professional levels? The CFO collaborates closely with you to carry out the company's vision and goals, while the controller and CFO work together to maintain strict standards for accurate financial data. For understanding and reporting on the operational, financial, and GAAP ends, the controller is equally crucial.

2. Keep up a reliable system for financial reporting.: It is essential to emphasise this. Ensuring the correctness of the income statement and balance sheet—which accounts for assets, liabilities, and equity—is part of maintaining a precise and timely reporting structure. The income statement and forecasted levels suffer from disorganised and jumbled financials.

If the idea of dealing with your complicated finances overwhelms you, think about getting outside financial assistance from a professional. Your financial data will be improved and your work will be much reduced if you outsource the process of setting up procedures.

Remember that the KPIs you choose are critical to the success of your company strategy. Metrics that are excellent for eCommerce might not be as applicable to companies in the food services sector. Additionally, a lot of owners often fail to see how crucial it is to have the appropriate technology in place for financial operations. Owners may lose out on technologies like Quickbooks or NetSuite that can automate a lot of financial processes, especially if they don't have a CFO or controller on staff. Be open-minded about potential technology and tool investments that might help your financial staff.

3. Both short- and long-term planning: "We all need lots of powerful long-range goals to help us past the short-term obstacles," remarked Jim Rohn, a successful businessman. Together, short- and long-term planning enable us to accomplish our overarching corporate objectives. Leveraging your company's advantages and KPIs as you align to your overall strategy plan is the basis of both long- and short-term planning.

Depending on the stage of growth of a firm, long-term planning might mean different things (up to six months for startups and two to three years for bigger organisations). As you prepare, refer to your annual company strategy. How could sales resources and employee efforts contribute to your growth? What potential external or internal influences could affect your plans? How are you going to go about getting money? In order to determine your long-term plans in line with your strategy, these questions will be useful.

The main focus of short-term planning is probable negative occurrences and situations that might affect the company (such as financial difficulties, unexpected costs, or other events). Your financial statistics should, as usual, show the results of your planning and strategy. Even while you can't fully forecast the tides of economic change on an annual or quarterly basis, having a backup plan in place for things like more financial hardship and capital raises will be crucial to your company's ability to survive.

Financial modelling is an important component of both short- and long-term planning. Financial modelling sets the stage and serves as a sandbox for you to detect distinct results and make modifications to present operations. It is essential to understanding timelines and financial performance at any future time period. Based on current performance, it generates insights for current financial planning and assists you in identifying potential roadblocks.

Although these three actions are simple, they are essential to maintaining a well-functioning financial system. But don't think you have to handle everything by yourself. Securing skilled assistance from a certified finance specialist might relieve some of your burden. When difficulties arise, you will be better equipped to respond with confidence if you work to strengthen your team, plan wisely, and correctly communicate your findings.

Exploring Financial Options: Bootstrapping, Loans, Grants And Investor Funding

Establishing a business is a thrilling endeavour that demands a lot of effort, commitment, and capital. When launching a business, one of the most crucial things to think about is funding.

Bootstrapping

Due to its low expenses, bootstrapping is a common choice for business owners starting a new venture. This tactic entails using credit cards and savings accounts as the main sources of personal money for the company. An entrepreneur who bootstraps their company may make all of the choices for it without having to answer to partners or outside investors.

Through bootstrapping, the startup maintains total control over its operations and costs while still having the funds available to spend in critical areas of the company that will support its expansion.

Additionally, bootstrapping enables business owners to retain a larger portion of their company's ownership, which may be advantageous should they want to go public in the future.

Furthermore, it enables them to establish rapport with their clients and gain a deeper understanding of them prior to launching extensive marketing initiatives. One drawback of bootstrapping is that it reduces the amount of money available for investments in potential development opportunities, including entering new markets or recruiting important employees. To guarantee success in certain situations, additional funding sources could be required. But when done right, bootstrapping can give entrepreneurs a solid platform on which to build their companies and expand.

Both venture capitalists and investors

These forms of funding entail investors giving businesses money in return for stock or a portion of the company. Due to their direct involvement, angel investors often provide less cash than venture capitalists but have more control over the strategy and day-to-day operations of the firm.

Conversely, venture capitalists often make substantial investments but are less involved in day-to-day operations. Entrepreneurs can also benefit greatly from the assistance of angel and venture capitalists, who can help them decide on business strategy and expansion prospects.

Grants and Loans

Getting a grant or loan from a bank is an additional choice for entrepreneurs. Generally speaking, grants and loans are given to businesses who can prove they have the resources to pay back the grants or loans and can manage the cash responsibly. Due to interest rates, bank loans are frequently more expensive than alternative financing choices, but they can be advantageous for business owners seeking greater quantities of money and longer payback terms. However, in the quick-paced world of the internet, there are many online lenders who provide more flexible loan conditions for startups, such as Lendly (which is comparable to Lendly).

Conversely, grants can offer significant financial support without requiring repayment of debt. Typically, grants are provided by governmental or nonprofit entities to encourage creative and good social projects.

It might be difficult for a startup to choose the best funding solution, but by being aware of the advantages of each, business owners can make well-informed selections. For new businesses, bootstrapping is typically the ideal option since it offers total control over operations at low overhead expenses. Obtaining investments from venture capitalists or investors may be a better option for individuals wishing to acquire greater sums of money or benefit from mentorship possibilities. In the meanwhile, people who want to fund certain initiatives without incurring debt might benefit from grants and loans. The ideal finance solution ultimately depends on the objectives and unique requirements of a firm.

Crafting A Persuasive Pitch Deck: Capturing Investor Attention And Funding

Crucial Dos and Don'ts for Pitch Decks for Investors

Prior to delving into the essential components of a successful investment pitch deck, allow us to emphasise a few crucial dos and don'ts that you should bear in mind while you create your captivating presentation.

Do: Clearly State the Issue and Its Fix

A vital "do" for your investor pitch deck is to state the problem your product or service solves succinctly and to offer an engaging fix. Investors must comprehend the problems faced by your target market and how your offering offers a special and worthwhile remedy. After stating the issue in clear and convincing terms, describe how your company plans to address it. You will draw potential investors' attention and interest by demonstrating a clear problem-solution fit.

Do: Highlight Market Possibilities and Opportunities

Investing opportunities with substantial market potential and room for growth are always sought after by investors. Emphasise the size and characteristics of your target market in your pitch deck, along with significant trends and data that bolster its allure. Talk about your industry's competitive environment and show that you have a thorough understanding of it. You can give investors confidence that they are investing in a profitable venture by demonstrating the market opportunity and potential of your business.

Do: Make a compelling value argument.

Your pitch deck's central focus is your value proposition. Clearly state how your company differs from the competition and why customers should select your goods or service. Emphasise the special qualities, advantages, and benefits that make your product or service alluring. To properly communicate the value your company offers, use compelling storytelling and imagery. To draw in investors and persuade them of the profitability and scalability of your business, you must have a compelling value proposition.

Avoid: Packing the Deck with Too Much Information

While it's important to include pertinent information, try not to stuff your design pitch deck with too much information. Make sure it's clear, concise, and visually appealing. To show important data points and draw attention to the most crucial elements of your company, use charts, graphics, and bullet points. Keep in mind that your pitch deck should act as a hook to pique interest and encourage more conversation. Instead of giving investors too much information at once, make time for questions and start a dialogue.

Avoid: Ignore a Forceful Call to Action

It's simple to overlook the significance of a compelling call-to-action (CTA) in your pitch deck during the thrill of showcasing your company. Clearly state what you want from investors in terms of money, collaborations, or additional conversations. Motivate them to show interest in contacting you or take the next step. A well-written CTA advances the conversation and guarantees that investors understand how to interact with you.

You can build an engaging investor pitch deck that successfully conveys the value of your company, draws in investors, and raises your chances of getting the capital and assistance you require for the success of your startup by following these dos and don'ts.

Which Slides Should You Include Most Importantly in Your Investor Pitch Deck?

It's crucial to include key slides in your investor pitch deck that succinctly communicate the most important details of your company. Potential investors are drawn in and interested by the thorough summary these slides offer.

1. Overview of the Company

Give a brief synopsis of your company's past, accomplishments, and history to introduce it. Emphasise noteworthy accomplishments, including noteworthy client acquisitions, accolades, or partnerships. Share what makes your business distinct and what makes it stand out.

2. The Company's Mission and Vision

Describe the goals and objectives of your business. Communicate your long-term objectives and core values, as well as the direction and purpose of your company. Give a convincing account of the future you want to build and how your business will appeal to investors with similar beliefs.

3. The Group

Present the important players on your team, emphasising their accomplishments, experience, and area of specialty. Emphasise their responsibilities and the ways in which their abilities support the growth of your company. Investors want to see a strong, competent staff leading the business.

4. The Issue

Clearly state the issue or pain point that your intended audience is experiencing. Show the gravity and importance of the issue with facts and real-world situations. This slide provides the framework for demonstrating the importance and suitability of your offering.

5. The Resolution

Give a presentation of your fix for the noted issue. Describe how your offering successfully resolves the issues that your target market is experiencing. Emphasise the special qualities and advantages of your solution and show how it performs better than the competition.

6. The Prospects for the Market

Showcase your target market's size, growth potential, and characteristics. Present significant market trends, data, and forecasts to highlight the appeal and expandability of your company. Make sure you communicate the market potential that investing in your business will provide for investors.

7. The End Item

Give a brief demonstration of your offering and its functionality. For effective product communication, use prototypes, images, or product demonstrations to highlight features and benefits. Emphasise any innovations and USPs that set your product apart from the competition.

8. The Clientele

Describe the needs and pain points of the target client segments. Showcase how your offering fulfils their needs and improves their quality of life. To establish credibility, share case studies, partnerships, or consumer testimonials from the past.

9. The Technological

Emphasise the technology that powers your offering, if appropriate. Describe any unique or exclusive features that provide you a competitive edge. Highlight your technological know-how and how it affects your market position and future growth.

10. The Rivalry

Recognize your rivals and have a deep comprehension of the market environment. Emphasise the unique selling points of your company and the reasons clients select your solution over competitors. Highlight the distinctive value you offer and any entrance obstacles that provide you a competitive advantage.

11. Steering

Talk about any noteworthy successes, benchmarks, or traction your company has achieved. This could involve reaching milestones in product development, forming strategic alliances, increasing revenue, or acquiring customers. Traction gives prospective investors confidence by proving validation and advancement.

12. Company Overview

Give a detailed description of your business plan, including your revenue sources, price policies, and distribution routes. Describe the revenue-generating strategies your organisation uses and its intentions for achieving profitability. Outline a precise plan for achieving scalability and sustainability.

13. The Plan for Marketing:

Give an explanation of your marketing and customer-acquisition tactics. Describe your strategy for reaching your target audience, spreading awareness, and encouraging customer uptake. Describe your go-to-market plan and any creative marketing campaigns that make you stand out.

14. Cash

Give a summary of your financial predictions, including timetables for profitability, significant financial KPIs, and revenue projections. Please include any historical growth or financial performance. The financial sustainability and possible return on investment for investors are shown on this slide.

15. The Request

At the end of your investor pitch decks, make it apparent what you want in return. Whether it's a precise financing amount, industry connections, or strategic partnership, make your task direct and unambiguous. Urge prospective investors to join you on your business journey by following these steps.

Be Sure to Examine Additional Pitch Decks As an illustration: It's critical to take inspiration from effective examples in order to produce an investor pitch deck that stands out. Examining previous pitch decks can provide important insights into what makes a good design, layout, and content.

Spend some time looking over and analysing the pitch decks of both new and established businesses. Seek out illustrations that speak to your target market or industry. Determine which pitch decks have attracted attention from the entrepreneurial community or obtained funding. You can get ideas for your presentation and have a better understanding of what works effectively by dissecting these decks.

Examine the Content, Design, and Structure

Examine other pitch decks and take note of their general layout, visual components, and content. Watch how they draw the audience in and keep the presentation moving in a logical manner. To improve the visual appeal, take into account utilising images, graphics, and typography. Examine how they employ storytelling strategies, display facts, and successfully communicate their value. Make a note of any original or imaginative methods that hold the audience's attention.

It's important to take inspiration from pitch decks that have been successful, but don't forget to modify the ideas and concepts to suit your company and sector. Modify the content, design components, and structure to fit your target market, value proposition, and market. Being genuine and unique is essential to making your pitch deck stand out, so refrain from directly duplicating or mimicking other people's work. Rather, make a presentation that truly captures the essence and advantages of your company using the inspiration as a guide.

Navigating The Legal Implications: Understanding Business Structures, Taxes And Regulations

A new company must choose a corporate structure at the outset, which will have an impact on taxes and the law. Additionally, selecting a business structure is a crucial first step for a startup. It may have an impact on liability, recurring expenses, and the composition of your business team. Because your business's structure has immediate tax ramifications, this topic becomes more relevant during tax season.

A Business Structure: What Is It?

One kind of a business's legal organisation is its structure. Selecting the appropriate business entity type requires careful consideration when launching a new company. Your choice of business structure will not affect how your company operates on a daily basis, but it will play a major role in identifying ownership, limiting personal liability, handling business taxes, and planning for future expansion.

Business entities, in essence, create the business as a separate legal entity that is capable of conducting business, entering into contracts, and opening bank accounts without having to use your own name for everything. Working under your own name might be acceptable for some very small enterprises, but it's probably advisable to select a business structure and register with your state if you intend to recruit staff, sign contracts, or make a full-time living from the venture.

One type of legal arrangement for a business is a business structure.

Personal liability protection and other advantages could be provided by the appropriate corporate structure.

Most companies need to register with their state and select a business structure.

Every form of business structure has advantages and disadvantages exclusive to its own kind.

A Variety of Business Structures:

1. Individual business ownership:

One of the most prevalent forms of business structures is the sole proprietorship. A lone proprietor is "someone who owns an unincorporated business by himself or herself," according to the IRS(opens in new tab). A sole proprietorship's main benefit is its simplicity. Since there is no separation in this case between the firm and its owner, the owner is entitled to all profits. It also implies that the lone owner bears full liability for all debts, losses, and liabilities of the company. This implies that in the event that the business accounts are insufficient to pay the obligation, creditors or lawsuit claimants may be able to seek the business owner's personal assets and accounts. Independent consultants, teachers, caterers, and freelance writers are a few examples of sole proprietorships.

An overview of the liabilities that arise from doing business.

A corporate loss under a limited liability structure cannot be more than the capital contributed to a partnership or LLC. To put it another way, if the business fails, the private assets of the owners and investors are safe. Therefore, personal assets are untouchable in a lawsuit against a limited liability business; the plaintiffs are suing the firm.

On the other hand, personal liability occurs when a business owner's assets are used to pay off any debt the company may have.

However, "piercing the corporate veil" is the most popular method of debt settlement used by close corporations, and it can happen in cases of grave misbehaviour. In this situation, courts disregard limited liability and hold stockholders of a company accountable for the deeds or debts of the firm on an individual basis.

❖ entity that passes across

Sole ownerships are viewed as "go through substances" for charge purposes. This type of structure, which also goes by the names "flow-through entity" and "fiscally transparent entity," denotes that the company does not pay taxes. Charges are "went through" to the proprietor all things being equal. Corporate income tax does not apply to pass-through organisations. Profits flow through to owners, who on Tax Day, often April 15, pay them at regular income tax rates in their personal returns.

Entity that passes across Benefits:

- You are a sole proprietor by default and there is no startup cost.
- Simple to maintain: Starting, operating, and ending a sole proprietorship does not involve any continuing registration or regulatory requirements.
- entity that passes across Cons: Personal liability: You bear personal responsibility for any mishap involving the company.
- No advantages to taxes: You must use Schedule to include company earnings on your personal tax return and pay self-employment tax on all earnings.

- Not as polished: Customers and clients can perceive you as unprofessional if your company isn't properly registered. It could be difficult for you to obtain business funding.

2. Collaboration

A partnership is defined as "the relationship existing between two or more persons who join to carry on a trade or business" in terms of business structure (opens in new tab). A general partnership, limited partnership, or limited liability partnership are the three primary categories for partnerships.

A general partnership is made up of two or more people who equally share all obligations and liabilities. This indicates that both partners are involved in the day-to-day management of the company. It also implies that all obligations incurred by the company would be equally borne by the partners. "General partners" refers to each and every partner.

- ❖ Limited Liability Partnership (LP): consists of at least one "limited partner" and one "general partner." A general partner takes on limitless liability as well as control of the company's activities. A silent partner, sometimes referred to as a limited partner, contributes money to the company. Limited partners do, however, have limited liability because they are not involved in day-to-day operations and do not have voting rights(opens in new tab).

- ❖ Partnership with limited liability (LLP): All partners in this arrangement have limited personal liability, which shields them from blame for malpractice or carelessness committed by other partners. An LLP allows for the management of the company to be shared by all of its members. Because partners are free to choose their own management structure, it is typically more adaptable than earlier partnership types.

In terms of taxes, partnerships are regarded as pass-through entities, just like sole proprietorships are. A partnership has similarities to an enlarged sole proprietorship, albeit with the benefits and drawbacks of having a partner. A partner can give the company finance, knowledge, and abilities. They may have a beneficial effect on the company, but they may also have a negative one. Whenever you do business with someone, you should feel at ease with them.

The fifteenth day of the third month following the conclusion of the entity's tax year, usually on March 15 or March 16 in the year, is when partnership tax returns are due. Despite the fact that the taxes are filed in March, partners typically wait to pay business taxes until the April deadline, which falls on July 15 of each year, because the business taxes flow through to their personal tax returns.

Advantages of Partnerships:

- comparatively simple to make: Forming an alliance with your state is a rather easy procedure.
- Potentially provide liability defences: There may be financial and legal liability protection available to individuals through limited partnerships and limited liability partnerships.

Cons of Partnerships:

- May not provide complete liability protection: Depending on the particular firm structure and practices, partnerships may not provide complete liability protection.
- More intricate tax regulations: partnerships are required to submit their own tax returns

and give partners extra paperwork to complete for personal taxes.

3. Limited liability business

The issue that starts to become a bit questionable is when you go into an LLC. According to the IRS, an LLC is a "business structure permitted by state rule." This indicates that it is constituted in accordance with state law, and that state laws pertaining to LLCs differ. The IRS will consider an LLC as either a corporation, partnership, or as part of the LLC's owner's tax return (i.e., a "disregarded entity(opens in new tab)" with many traits similar to a sole proprietorship), depending on the elections made by the LLC and its features.

Because it can have characteristics of many different corporate forms based on the decisions made by the owners, an LLC is regarded as a hybrid legal entity. Compared to some of its competitors in business structures, this gives it greater safeguards and flexibility. Members of a limited liability company are not held personally accountable. The LLC has flexibility when it comes to its federal tax status because it is an entity established by state statute. For example, a single-member LLC (opens in new tab) may be subject to corporation or sole proprietorship taxes. A multi-member LLC (opens in a new tab) may be subject to corporation or partnership taxes.

Regarding the federal tax due date, there are certain disparities as a result of the previously indicated flexibility.

The federal tax filing and payment deadline for an LLC that elects to be treated as a sole proprietorship or C corporation (more on C corporation forms below) is usually April 15.

On the other hand, an LLC that is subject to S corporation or partnership taxes would normally have a payment deadline that corresponds with their individual income return and a federal tax filing deadline of March 15.

Limited Liability Corporation Advantages:

❖ Protection against liability for one or more owners: An LLC provides liability protection for its owners, including a single owner, when it is set up and run properly.

❖ Select one of two taxation strategies: Choose the tax structure that will work best for owner finances: S Corp taxation or pass-through taxation.

❖ Possibility of significant tax savings: S Corp taxation may reduce self-employment taxes for owners who work in the company full-time.

Limited Liability Corporation Cons:

- Establishing and maintaining an LLC costs money because it involves filing paperwork with the government and paying fees.
- More complicated tax requirements: If you choose S Corp taxes, there may be more complicated tax preparation.

4. Business

Companies or groups of persons with the authority to operate as a single legal body are known as corporations. This indicates that there is no personal liability because the business is seen as distinct from its owners. Nonetheless, a company is sometimes referred to as a "legal person" since it is qualified for many of the same rights as an individual.(new tab opens) For example, a company has the right to free expression, can enter into contracts, and can sue or be sued.

Corporations are divided by the IRS into two distinct categories: "C corporations" and "S corporations."

Company C (C corp): The default designation for corporations is thought to be C corporation. When submitting their articles of incorporation to the state's business filing office, all corporations are first classified as "C" entities. C corporations differ from our previous corporate models in that they are not pass-through entities. Double taxation occurs when they are subject to both corporate and personal income taxes.

❖ double taxation

S corporation (S corp): Because a S corporation is a pass-through entity and can avoid double taxation, it differs noticeably from a C corporation. But the IRS has tight guidelines(opens in a new tab) for businesses wishing to become S corporations, especially with regard to stockholders. An S corporation, for example, is limited to 100 stockholders, all of whom must be citizens or residents of the United States. (It's common for startups to issue 100,000 shares of stock at launch; it opens in a new tab).

Similar to partnerships, S corporations are required to file their annual federal tax returns by the fifteenth day of the third month, usually on March 15, after the end of the tax year. Following that, the money is distributed to each member's individual returns, which follow the regular April Tax Day schedule.

The only business tax structure that permits perpetual existence is the corporation tax structure. This indicates that the arrival and departure of shareholders, officers, and directors has no bearing on its ability to continue.

Business Advantages:

Broad liability protections: If the business is run properly, shareholders who own S Corp and C Corp companies are entitled to broader legal protection.

A company has the same legal rights as an individual person, including the ability to enter into contracts and conduct business.

Unlimited number of shareholders are permitted for S corporations; the maximum number is 100. Shareholders in C corporations are not limited in number.

Business Cons: Costlier to create and maintain: Creating and maintaining a corporation usually involves more work and money.

Specific continuous obligations: State-imposed rules, yearly meetings, and the appointment of a board of directors are just a few of the requirements that corporations must comply with.

Managing Financial Resources Effectively: Implementing, Budgeting, Accounting And Cash Flow Management

Financial management: what is it?

Financial management is essentially the process of creating a business plan and then making sure every department follows it. A long-term vision may be created with the help of solid financial management, which also makes it possible for the CFO or VP of finance to present statistics on liquidity, profitability, cash runway, and other topics.

Finance teams can accomplish these objectives with the aid of ERP software: Several financial tasks, including accounting, fixed-asset management, revenue recognition, and payment processing, are combined into a financial management system. Through the integration of these essential elements, a financial management system guarantees instantaneous insight into an organisation's financial condition and streamlines routine tasks, such as period-end close procedures.

The Financial Management Objectives

1. Building upon these foundations, finance managers support their organisations in a number of ways, such as but not restricted to:
2. Optimising profits: Share information on factors that could cause the cost of items supplied to rise, such as growing raw material costs.
3. Monitoring cash flow and liquidity: Make sure the business has adequate cash on hand to pay its debts.
4. Maintaining compliance: Comply with all applicable state, federal, and industry regulations.

   Creating monetary scenarios Based on the company's present situation and projections that take a broad variety of prospective market situations into account, these are made.

5. Handle relationships: Interacting with boards of directors and investors in an efficient manner.

Financial Management's Scope

Four primary domains are included in financial management:

1. Organizing

The financial manager forecasts the amount of money the business will require to keep a positive cash flow, allot funds for expansion or the addition of new goods or services, and deal with unforeseen circumstances. They then share this information with other business partners.

There are various categories into which planning can be divided, such as capital expenses, labour and expenses, and indirect and operating expenses.

2. Establishing a budget

The company's available money is distributed by the financial management to cover expenses like rent or mortgage payments, payroll, raw materials, employee T&E, and other commitments. Ideally, some will remain to save for unexpected expenses and to finance potential new ventures.

Businesses often have a master budget, as well as smaller, more focused papers that address specific topics like cash flow and operations. Master budgets can be fixed or variable.

3. Managing and evaluating risk:

Financial managers are tasked by line-of-business leaders with evaluating and providing compensating controls for a range of risks, such as:

Market risk influences the company's stock performance, reporting, and investments. It also affects public firms. could also be a reflection of industry-specific financial risk, such a pandemic that affects eateries or the transition of retail to a direct-to-consumer business model.

4. Credit danger

The consequences of, say, late payments from clients, which leave the company unable to pay its debts and could have a negative impact on creditworthiness and valuation—factors that determine an organisation's capacity to borrow money at reasonable interest rates.

5. Risk to liquidity

Teams in charge of finance must monitor cash flow, project cash requirements for the future, and be ready to release working capital when required.

Risk associated with operations

This is a broad category that several financial teams are unfamiliar with. It might address things like the possibility of a cyberattack, whether to get cybersecurity insurance, what preparations are in place for disaster recovery and business continuity, and what crisis management procedures are activated in the event that a senior leader is charged with fraud or other wrongdoing.

6. Operations

The finance manager establishes guidelines for the secure and accurate processing and distribution of financial data, such as invoices, payments, and reports, by the finance team. These documented procedures also specify who within the company is in charge of making financial decisions and who approves them.

Businesses don't have to start from scratch because a range of organisation kinds have policy and procedure templates accessible, like this one for NGOs.

Chapter 4

Building a Team of Passion And Expertise: Assembling Your Dream Team

Team development: what is it?

The process of bringing different people together to create a productive team is known as team development. Effective teams must be able to collaborate well in order for individuals to contribute as much as possible to the team's goal.

However, it involves more than just putting disparate people in a group and assigning them a task or objective.

Leadership that is inclusive, purposeful, and nurturing is necessary for team development. In addition, each team member and the leader must possess a certain amount of self-awareness. What qualities does each person possess? In what ways might the strengths of one member enhance the opportunities of another? How can a leader enable every member of the team to realise their own potential?

Think about the position of the leader when you're trying to build a new team or improve the one you already have. Teams with effective leaders are typically successful.

Future-focused executives have a tremendous amount of influence on an organisation, as we have discovered. What is meant by that? Prospective leaders know how to use prospection. Each of us has the capacity for prospect, which is the ability to consider the future and imagine what might be. It requires a blend of practicality, optimism, and the capacity to consider other scenarios.

What was the outcome? Teams are more creative, dynamic, and nimble. Additionally, we've discovered that teams are more risk-taking, resilient, and productive.

While you're building teams, think about how your company can develop its leaders. Your organisation will benefit greatly from investing in your team leaders' competencies.

Eleven competencies are required for team building

The key components of effective team development are a few specific abilities.

- Solving issues
- Robust and transparent communication
- Relationship- or interpersonal-building abilities
- Time management
- Hearing, particularly attentive hearing
- Capacity to establish objectives and assess them

- Providing and getting comments
- Project oversight
- Aptitude for organisation
- An attitude of growth
- Team coherence

It's critical to consider each team member as a whole when building your team. Each person has a different viewpoint and set of abilities. To have the most impact, think about how you can utilise each teammate's potential. You'll also position yourself for greater team management abilities by doing this.

Seven Strategies to Grow your Team

On your team, there may be a few recent hires in new positions. You may be putting together a new team composed of members from different departments inside your company. Alternatively, you may be assembling a brand-new team from the ground up and partnering them with a few seasoned teammates.

There are actions you must take to properly develop your team, regardless of where you are in the process of team-building. As the team leader, think about implementing these strategies.

- Determine your leadership and working style.
- Clearly define expectations, roles, and responsibilities.
- Encourage your group to make wise choices.
- Promote feedback and active listening.
- Encourage inclusivity, belonging, and trust.
- Promote a growing mentality.
- Give guidance.

1. Determine your leadership and working style:

It requires some introspection and self-awareness to take this first step. As a leader, you should examine yourself to see how you operate. What kind of input have you previously received that could assist you in determining your leadership style? Which method of working has helped you produce the most?

2. Clearly define positions, duties, and expectations:

A little bit of clarification helps a lot. Make sure everyone in the team is aware of their duties. It's also critical for leaders to express their expectations in a clear and concise manner.

Your staff will feel more empowered if roles and duties are clearly defined. Your team will be successful if you have clear goals and expectations for them.

3. Encourage your group to make wise choices:

Amazing things may occur when you place your team in charge. One of the most crucial aspects of building a team is giving your members decision-making authority. Leaders must think about the areas in which they can assign decision-making authority for various project components.

4. Promote feedback and attentive listening:

A team's leader must be able to listen well. Leaders that pay attention to their teams have more developed teams, particularly in this digital age. It demonstrates your compassion and empathetic nature. However, it also demonstrates your efforts to comprehend your team and the difficulties they can encounter.

Giving and accepting feedback is an essential part of any team dynamic, just like listening is. Actually, according to 65% of workers, they would prefer to get more input.

The benefits of feedback for team development are numerous. It demonstrates maturity and confidence, for instance. Additionally, it fosters a culture in which criticism is accepted and valued.

It can dispel that feeling of anxiety and encourage constructive discussion and collaboration. Finally, it may pave the way for a greater sense of self-awareness.

5. Promote inclusivity, belonging, and trust:

Teams that have members that have a sense of belonging do better than those that don't. Indeed, we've observed the following outcomes in teams led by inclusive leaders:

Workers are 50% more efficient

Workers are 90% more creative

Workers are 150% more involved.

Additionally, inclusive leadership reduces employee turnover by 54%. From the start, cultivate a strong sense of inclusivity, trust, and belonging.

6. Promote a mindset of progress:

Employees need to have a growth attitude if you want them to succeed. If you have a growth mentality, you can enhance your skills and abilities by working hard and being dedicated. A growth mentality is the capacity to look beyond the limited, static experience of the present.

Businesses that embrace a growth mentality frequently give employees greater opportunities to learn and develop. Searching for inspiration to get going? Your team's growth mentality will expand thanks to these 13 suggestions.

7. Offer guidance

Amazing things can happen to those who have access to individualised coaching. First, coaching promotes mental health among your staff. Teams with high mental fitness have a 31% increase in productivity. It also implies that workers are less likely to quit on their own volition and are more likely to recover from losses.

Personalised coaching boosts self-awareness, resilience, and teamwork, but it also strengthens mental fitness. After working with a coach for just three months, Better Up members report a 38% reduction in languishing.

Which 5 Phases make up Team Development?

Every team goes through developmental phases. Bruce Tuckman's five phases of team growth, which were developed in the 1960s, are still helpful, albeit not exhaustive. Every stage is unique and has its own emotions and actions.

As you grow as a leader, it's critical to understand the phases of your team.

1. Establishing

The formation phase starts at the time the team is first formed. Colleagues are paired off and begin getting to know one another. Employees frequently experience a mix of exhilaration and anxiety at this point.

Employees should take this opportunity to get to know one another's hobbies, backgrounds, and skill sets. Project goals and deadlines should be communicated by the team leader. The tasks and responsibilities of each team member should be clearly defined by the leader. Ascertain that you're holding frequent team meetings and encouraging effective, transparent communication.

2. Arresting

At this point in the team's development, there may be some conflict among the staff. There may be difficulties during the storming phase, particularly with regard to project strategy. This is frequently the result of disparities in personality and methods of operation. It's typical for teammates to become irritated.

However, it is vitally necessary for leaders to assist team members in managing conflict in an efficient manner. The team leader's job is to aid team members with any discomfort they may be experiencing and to clear up any misunderstandings. However, it's equally critical for team members and leaders to respect and value one another's differences.

The group must learn to accommodate these differences and embrace constructive conflict in a way that upholds dedication to the group's goals and trust.

3. Establishing Norms

This stage of team building is sometimes referred to as "getting into the groove." If members of your team start pointing out each other's strengths, your team has entered the norming phase. During this stage, staff members will also start to comprehend one another's responsibilities and feel more at ease collaborating.

You will probably notice that staff members begin to socialise more during this phase. It's also possible that colleagues will feel more at ease approaching you for comments or guidance.

It's critical for leaders to ensure that any buried conflicts don't fester without a determined attempt to address them. It's crucial for project managers to communicate deliverables and expectations and to stay up to speed on project updates.

4. Executing

Employees are accustomed to working side by side by this point. They've probably developed close bonds and learned how to collaborate most effectively.

This is what we like to refer to as the "peak performance" phase of team growth. Teams are most productive at this point because they are collaborating swiftly to reach the final goal.

This could be an excellent time to offer coaching or mentoring programs. With individualised assistance, your team will keep developing and expanding.

5. Closing

This completes the team development process. Employees move on to other projects during the adjourning phase, which is often referred to as the mourning period. The group has achieved the goals it set out to achieve.

Employees who have attained their last aim typically feel happy, successful, and excited. But throughout this time, they have also developed solid professional and interpersonal ties. Workers may also express regret and disappointment that this experience is over.

Recognizing employees is essential at this point. It is crucial for a leader to acknowledge and value the team's efforts and contributions. It's a wonderful opportunity to honour the team and inspire coworkers to honour one another.

The team may never reach the adjourning stage if it is not project-based. For instance, only a worker who has made the decision to depart the team in favour of a new position may enter the adjourning phase. Alternatively, another worker may decide to quit the organisation entirely.

Nevertheless, it's critical to acknowledge and value the team's contributions at every stage of the project.

creating teams that laugh together

How to keep your group together

These days, everyone is talking about employee retention. Given the historically high rate of employee turnover, it is evident that retention techniques are a primary priority for businesses.

Here are six strategies to think about if you're a leader trying to keep your team members happy while also retaining them.

Ensure that every worker has a strong sense of belonging: One of the most important predictors of an employee's decision to remain with a company is their sense of belonging.

Demonstrate inclusive leadership abilities: Workers under inclusive leaders experience 90% more team innovation and 140% more team engagement. Additionally, inclusive leader teams perform better than non-inclusive leader teams. Additionally, inclusive leaders observe a 54% decrease in team turnover.

Permit workers to develop and learn: As previously said, team development depends on having a growth attitude. Give staff members the chance to develop new skills and apply their existing ones in order to learn and advance. You can provide team-building activities centred on mutual education.

Give your staff recognition frequently: Employee gratitude makes a big difference. In actuality, acknowledgment improves the performance of your company. Higher employee happiness, a stronger feeling of purpose, and higher retention rates are the results.

Learn to know the people in your team personally. It may seem obvious, yet some leaders forget this important aspect. People are more likely to experience a sense of belonging to the team and organisation when they perceive their leaders to be concerned and empathetic toward them. Virtual team-building exercises can help you get to know your team—and help them get to know you—even in remote or hybrid work contexts.

Put the team's mental health and well-being first: It is crucial to be mentally fit, especially in light of all the uncertainties. Put the health of your team first and provide chances, such as coaching, for mental fitness development.

Identifying key Roles: Recruiting Talent that Aligns with your Business Needs

It's critical now more than ever for businesses to accurately describe their job descriptions and match them with the right people when it comes to filling positions involving financial functions. By doing this, the company not only increases the pool of qualified applicants but also guarantees that those hired possess the knowledge, expertise, and work ethic needed to succeed in the position. Learn how to create job descriptions that are appropriate and match them with the right applicants.

1. Determine the Principal Duties

Determining the primary duties of the position is the first stage in creating a job description. This entails considering the responsibilities and daily tasks that the worker will be expected to carry out. The job description should include a clear and succinct outline of these essential duties. For instance, jobs pertaining to accounting may involve duties like creating financial statements, overseeing accounts payable, and more.

2. Establish the Necessary Qualifications and Skills

Finding the necessary abilities and credentials for the position is the next stage. This entails considering what kind of schooling, experience, training, and certifications the perfect applicant should have. This is particularly crucial for positions in finance, since these workers deal with incredibly sensitive data and must be adequately trained and accredited to carry out certain tasks and projects in compliance with legal requirements. The job description should also include a list of these prerequisite knowledge and abilities.

3. Explain the company's values and culture.

The job description should include a description of the corporate culture and values in addition to the primary duties and necessary abilities. This contains details regarding the work environment, corporate culture, and the company's mission, vision, and values. These vital components will demonstrate to candidates how a company supports the development and success of its employees while also having an impact on the community. Candidates will be better able to determine if the company is a good fit for them by doing this.

4. Speak Clearly and Briefly

It's critical to utilise easy-to-understand language that is clear, short, and concise when drafting job descriptions. Steer clear of using excessively complex or technical terminology as this could turn off or confuse applicants. It can still be important to use certain role-specific language to ensure that candidates fully grasp the requirements of the position. It will be helpful to break up the information into brief paragraphs and bullet points.

5. Concentrate on Outcomes

It's crucial to pay attention to the outcomes the candidate should be able to accomplish in the role as well as the duties and responsibilities of the position. How can applicants for positions in finance provide fresh ideas and novel solutions to the team? Take into account how the position will affect the company's objectives and how the candidate will help to achieve them.

6. Evaluate and Enhance the Job Posting

Before posting the job description, it's crucial to go over and make any necessary revisions. This includes proofreading to ensure that all important duties and necessary abilities are covered, checking for typos, and ensuring that the language is clear and succinct.

Employers may draw in the best applicants and raise the chance of a successful hire by crafting job descriptions precisely and matching them with ideal individuals. It's crucial to take the time to carefully craft a job description that appropriately captures the essence of the position and the organisation, and to continuously evaluate and improve it to make sure it stays current.

Cultivating a Culture of Collaboration: Fostering Teamwork and Shared Vision

Establishing a collaborative culture can yield immense benefits for all those involved in the prosperity of an enterprise. Collaboration not only encourages employees to build trust and create innovative solutions, but it may also move organisational goals forward in ways that might not have been possible otherwise. Here are some basic actions you may take to facilitate good teamwork if you're interested in creating such a culture in your company.

What does a Collaborative Culture Entail?

A collaborative culture is a work environment that emphasises teamwork as a means of optimising employees' unique skill sets and competencies. Collaborative cultures thrive in organisations when team members are purposefully given the opportunity to regularly collaborate toward shared objectives. The fundamental tenet of collaborative cultures is that workers may generate better work overall when they pool their individual talents to work together.

Teams who are able to work well together are frequently more creative, productive, and communicative than those that operate alone. By focusing their efforts on the community, collaborative teams can provide more creative solutions.

As a result, companies with this kind of culture may find greater success than they otherwise could. Furthermore, collaborative cultures can support teams in building solid bonds based on trust and flexibility, which may enhance worker engagement and happiness.

Characteristics of a Cooperative Culture

It might be a difficult endeavour to integrate collaboration into your organisation's process. Numerous workplace elements support and foster a collaborative culture, enabling its development.

You should carefully incorporate these elements into the platforms that your teams utilise in order to foster innovation, creativity, and engagement in your workplace. The following seven characteristics of a strong and cooperative culture should be remembered:

Openness

Transparency is encouraged in the cultures of collaboration that are strongest. The teams in your firm should base every daily job on the principles of transparency. Encouraging transparency can make it easier for your team to reflect on procedures, build

162

skills, and learn from one another. It can also help shape responsibilities around specific, shared goals.

Leaders in organisations should also embrace the concept of transparency. Sharing thoughts from managers, particularly regarding organisational obstacles, helps foster a sense of inclusion among staff members in goal-oriented endeavours. Furthermore, people who are honest like this can improve their ability to reflect and solve problems.

Knowledge Dissemination

Knowledge sharing among team members to promote best practices and competency is a crucial component of collaborative cultures. This is difficult to do since, in conventional work settings, high-achieving personnel frequently exhibit reluctance to divulge to other team members the methods, strategies, and information that enable them to succeed.

Competitive work environments that reward individuals for their individual accomplishments rather than teams for their collective successes encourage this kind of behaviour. As a result, policies are usually in place in collaborative businesses to promote information exchange among staff members, which can assist make the most of the team's varying levels of experience.

Have Faith

Teams need to build a solid foundation of trust in order to cooperate effectively within your firm. In spite of this, managers frequently make the error of promoting cooperation without first establishing the kinds of connections necessary for productive teamwork. Only when members of the team have faith in one another to make constructive contributions to work procedures that advance the team's overall objectives can a strong culture of collaboration be developed.

Most people in collaborative environments agree that working together improves the calibre of output. Collaboration may quickly become the norm when staff members share a common knowledge of the goals they're aiming for and how they might work together to better achieve them.

Interaction

Nearly all successful firms are built on effective communication, but this is particularly true for those that foster collaborative environments. Team members need to be able to express their ideas and objectives through a variety of channels in order to function well together. Collaboration requires workers to regularly interact with supervisors, peers, and other organisational leaders. Employees can more easily coordinate operations and achieve organisational goals when they have improved communication abilities.

Purposeful Areas

A lot of cooperative businesses actively designate areas for teamwork to take place. These areas are frequently seen in cross-functional settings and are furnished with cosy furnishings, lots of room for interacting, and collaboratively-encouraging objects like whiteboards and computing gadgets. In essence, corporations utilise purposeful space creation as a tool to encourage team members to work together to develop creative solutions.

Objective Instruments and Tactics

Companies that foster a collaborative culture give their teams intentional tools and tactics. Technology-enabled collaboration solutions, including web-based workspaces, productivity apps, and cloud-based software, can enable staff members to work together virtually. Team members are more likely to utilise these tools faithfully and purposefully when they understand why they are utilising them and how they might advance organisational objectives. These tools are typically backed by the promotion of intentional techniques.

Participation

A hallmark of many effectively cooperative organisations is engagement. Team members may feel more energised and enthusiastic about their job when they can share visions and duties with others because collaboration is a very active and interactive endeavour. Moreover, cultures that prioritise cooperation tend to foster a sense of respect, value, and investment within their workforce, which can result in increased overall employee engagement.

How to foster a Culture of Cooperation at the Office

The precise procedures you should follow to establish a collaborative culture will likely vary depending on the kind of company you work for, how big it is, your workflow, and the sorts of cooperative frameworks you right now have set up. With that said, though, here are nine fundamental actions you can do to improve team collaboration and change business culture as a whole:

1. Describe your goal

Having a clear vision is the first step towards establishing a successful culture of collaboration in your company. When fostering a collaborative environment, it's important to comprehend and express your organisation's ultimate objective effectively. This vision should outline the specifics of collaboration, including how it will improve productivity inside your company and the actions you want to take to foster employees' capacity for collaboration.

To make sure that teamwork is a regular strategy, you need also think about how you will sustain the collaborative momentum within your company once it becomes the standard. After you've determined these elements, be sure to share your vision with your team. Leaders who set goals for their initiatives make it much simpler for team members to support the concept.

2. Look for cooperative leaders

Finding new leaders to take your firm through this cultural shift might be beneficial, even though you might be tempted to lead a cooperation program yourself. If there are outside candidates who have built successful collaborative cultures in other firms, you can think about hiring and developing them. These people may possess a particular managerial style, history, or tactical training method that can make it easier for your company to achieve its goals for teamwork.

After your tools for collaboration are set up and operating well, it's critical to recognize and commend leaders who firmly uphold the collaborative culture. This may encourage other leaders to make investments in teamwork as well.

3. Evaluate your present procedures

An essential step in creating a collaborative culture is evaluating the methods your company currently uses to reach goals. Examine these procedures to see where an excessive amount of independent work is being done. Once you identify processes that are focused on the individual, you can deliberately replace them with ones that promote teamwork.

Furthermore, in the course of your assessment, you ought to make an effort to identify procedures whose design may present possible obstacles to collaboration. Recognizing the shortcomings of your existing process can assist you in taking a more deliberate approach to putting collaborative solutions into practice.

4. Include chances for cooperation

It's crucial to realise that cooperation can only happen when you give your staff members the freedom to work together. If staff members are isolated in their offices and assigned separate tasks, it's unlikely that they will feel at ease utilising collaborative techniques to accomplish objectives. On the other hand, your team is more likely to adopt collaborative ways to achieve goals if you intentionally create opportunities for collaboration in your organisational workflow.

As a result, you should purposefully put workers in scenarios where teamwork is required. You can provide team members with opportunities to develop their collaborative abilities through the design of team projects, cross-functional task forces, organisational communication tools, coaching infrastructure, and small-group arrangements.

5. Unite your group.

As was already established, successful collaboration is built on trustworthy relationships. Colleagues are typically more successful in their teamwork when they have mutual trust and unite behind a common objective.

Your team has to be brought together to practise skills, bond, and form supportive relationships in order to develop trustworthy partnerships. This can be achieved by putting in place programs like organisational retreats, team-building exercises, professional development techniques, fun office activities, and more.

Furthermore, it is crucial to continuously strengthen the ties your team members have with one another once they have formed them. This can be achieved by giving staff members regular chances to interact socially and rewarding them when they do.

6. Accept diversity

When creating a successful collaborative culture, navigating differences in viewpoints and methods can be difficult. It's possible that some team members won't agree on how to best accomplish objectives, and it can take a while to acquire the abilities needed to compromise in this kind of situation.

As a result, it's critical that your collaborative culture welcomes diversity. It is important to acknowledge that disagreements will inevitably arise, but they shouldn't stop your company from moving forward. Framing differences in perspective as something that can help partners find answers they might not have separately can be tremendously helpful.

7. Provide rewards for teamwork and incentives

Your team is unlikely to find many incentives to collaborate if you encourage it but only give recognition to those who operate more independently. Therefore, it's critical to appropriately reward teamwork when fostering a collaborative atmosphere.

When staff members achieve a goal with exceptional work, don't forget to commend them for their particular collaboration. Offering monetary prizes or other incentives, such as time off or happy hours, is one way to recognize and reward joint achievements. Employees are more likely to take initiative seriously when they have goals to strive toward.

8. Establish feedback mechanisms

Establishing feedback mechanisms can assist you in monitoring organisational changes, including programs aimed at fostering culture. It's important to regularly assess how well your staff members are collaborating, and to step in when you see possible weaknesses in their methods.

You can utilise feedback software to take a more informal approach or enforce particular formal feedback cycles. By providing these feedback opportunities, you may improve the ease with which your staff members communicate about procedures and better support and foster collaboration within your company.

9. Make use of technology

Collaboration has been easier thanks to technology in recent years. You can assist your staff collaborate by providing them with digital tools like survey platforms, video-conferencing software, cloud-based productivity services, messaging apps, and more. The correct technology tools can enhance efficiency, productivity, and communication, giving your teams a general advantage when working together.

Nurturing Employee Growth and Development: Investing in Training and Career Advancement

The significance of staff training and development has risen to the top of corporate priorities in today's quickly changing business landscape. Companies all throughout the world are realising how important it is to invest in their personnel if they want to achieve long-term success as the competitive edge gets sharper. Initiatives for staff training and development have seen a notable surge in popularity; they are now essential for fostering innovation, growth, and employee engagement.

By providing workers with the information, abilities, and resources they require to succeed, companies boost their competitiveness and encourage a culture of ongoing team development. The advantages include lower attrition rates and increased morale and productivity.

Employee Training and Development: What Is It?

Employee training and development, or T&D for short, is a methodical organisational procedure designed to improve workers' performance in terms of knowledge, skills, and competences. It includes a range of educational opportunities and experiences intended to enable people to fulfil the demands of their current jobs and their long-term professional goals. Fundamentally, employee training gives workers the particular abilities and information needed to succeed in their present positions. This can include job-specific competencies, industry-specific knowledge, and technological proficiencies.

Employee development, on the other hand, goes beyond the demands of the job at hand, fostering a more comprehensive range of abilities and dispositions that can equip people for leadership positions in the future or flexibility in a workplace that is changing quickly. Good staff development and training programs are made to fit the specific needs of each person, in keeping with the organisation's strategic goals, and can be given in a variety of ways, including workshops, online courses, mentorship, or on-the-job training. Businesses may cultivate more proficient and driven teams and set themselves up for long-term success in a constantly changing business environment by investing in the training and development of their workforce.

The Advantages of Employee Development and Training

Employee development and training are crucial for both individuals and businesses. These programs act as stimulants to improve employees' knowledge and skill sets, enabling them to carry out their duties more accurately and efficiently. This ultimately results in fewer mistakes and a higher calibre of work. Training expenditures foster increased worker productivity. Their knowledge and abilities grow, enabling them to complete jobs faster and with better quality. The increased output results in financial benefits and improved operational effectiveness for the company.

The favourable effect on worker morale and job satisfaction is equally important. A company's employees feel loyal and satisfied when it provides them with growth chances. This reduces staff turnover, which is expensive for any company and improves job happiness at the same time. By identifying and developing future leaders within, internal development initiatives eliminate the need for costly external recruitment. These internal executives are familiar with the values and ethos of the organisation.

In the end, putting employee training and development first fosters creativity and adaptability within a company, strengthening its competitive advantage by enabling it to react quickly to changing market conditions and new trends.

Establishing Effective Communication Channels: Ensuring Transparency and Open Dialogue

Successful communication is essential in the fast-paced world of business. Transparency, open communication, and a cohesive work atmosphere can only be fostered through the establishment of clear and regular communication channels.

Facilitating unimpeded information exchange among departments, teams, and individuals can optimise workflow, avert miscommunications, and enable your team members to make well-informed decisions.

Determine Communication Needs: Determine the precise needs of your organisation before putting communication channels in place. Take into account your company's size and structure, the type of work you do, and the required frequency of communication. Determine the various kinds of information that must be exchanged and the best communication channels for each kind of information.

use the Right Channels: To accommodate a range of needs and preferences, use a number of communication channels. Think about utilising project management software, corporate intranets, email, instant messaging, video conferencing, and other modern and conventional communication techniques in conjunction.

Provide Explicit Communication recommendations: Formulate explicit recommendations about the use of various communication methods. Specify what is expected in terms of response times, privacy, and language usage. Make certain that every employee is aware of these rules and knows why each channel exists.

Encourage Honest and Open Communication: Encourage honest and open communication between all organisational levels. Establish a comfortable environment where staff members may express their opinions, raise worries, and ask questions without worrying about repercussions. Encourage a culture that values and responds to criticism.

Use Communication Channels Consistently: To uphold expectations and prevent misunderstandings, use communication channels consistently. Make sure that timely and frequent information sharing occurs. Don't over communicate with staff members, and give critical updates first priority.

Encourage Input and Adjustment: Ask staff members about their experiences using various channels of communication on a regular basis. Determine what needs to be improved upon and make the necessary changes. If implementing new technologies and techniques can improve the efficacy of communication, be open to doing so.

Educate Staff on Effective Communication Techniques: Train staff members on effective communication techniques. This could involve classes on how to use active listening techniques, write succinct and clear emails, and handle disagreements in a healthy way.

Set the example for effective communication as a leader by modelling it. Encourage individuals to communicate in an open and transparent manner by modelling this behaviour yourself. Set an example for empathy, constructive criticism, and active listening.

Monitor and Assess: Keep a regular eye on and assessment of your communication channels' efficacy. Evaluate the information flow, spot any gaps in communication, and take immediate action to resolve any issues or concerns.

You may empower your team members, promote a transparent culture, and propel your company forward by creating efficient communication channels. Recall that solid relationships, creativity, and expansion are all based on constant and open communication.

Advantages of Open Communication

Promotes open communication, more open collaboration, increased trust, more invention, and more idea sharing

Makes the workplace more knowledgeable

How to improve open lines of communication at work:

Notify co-workers or employees as soon as you learn of the information.

Respond to inquiries swiftly, truthfully, and with justifications.

Coordinate actions and communication with the unit's and the organisation's mission.

CHAPTER 5

Establishing a Robust Online Presence: Connecting With Your Target Audience

A good online presence is essential for any organisation to succeed in the modern digital era. Having a strong online presence enables you to establish a connection with your target market, advertise your goods and services, and raise brand awareness.

The following are essential actions for building a strong internet presence:

1. Identify Who Your Target Market Is

It's critical to identify your target audience precisely before you begin developing your internet presence. With your online marketing initiatives, who are you aiming to reach? What are their internet based propensities, leisure activities, and socioeconomics? You can adjust your content and marketing techniques after you have a clear understanding of your target audience.

2. Develop an Easy-to-Use Website

The groundwork of your web presence is your site. It ought to be intuitive to use, well-designed, and search engine optimised. Make sure your website has calls to action that are obvious and inspire users to take the next action, as well as a clear and appealing approach to exhibit your goods or services.

3. Create an Account on Social Media

Building relationships and establishing a connection with your target audience requires the use of social media. Select the social media channels that best suit your target market and industry, then produce interesting content that appeals to them. Share news, advertise goods and services, and engage with your fans on social media.

4. Participate in Virtual Communities

Engage in online forums that are pertinent to your target market and business. This could be posting comments on blogs, joining forums, or taking part in online chats. Participating in internet forums is a fantastic method to build your brand's reputation as a thought leader and make connections with prospective clients.

5. Make Use of Content Marketing

One effective strategy for drawing in and keeping your target audience is content marketing. Provide valuable, aesthetically pleasing content that speaks to their interests. Blog entries, articles, infographics, films, and podcasts may all fall under this category. Distribute your material on other websites and social media networks.

6. Make Search Engine Optimization

The practice of raising your website's position in search engine results pages (SERPs) is known as search engine optimization, or SEO. By doing this, you can increase the visibility of your website to prospective clients who are looking for information about your goods or services.

7. Manage Ads That Are Paid

Investing in paid advertising campaigns can help you reach a larger audience and increase website traffic. To target your ideal clients with relevant adverts, think about utilising platforms like Google adverts or social network advertising.

8. Track and Examine Your Outcomes

Keep an eye on the traffic to your website, the interaction on social media, and other indicators related to online marketing. This will assist you in identifying what is effective and what requires development. Over time, make use of this data to hone your tactics and enhance your web presence.

9. Adjust to Changing Internet Fashions

Since the internet market is always evolving, it's critical to keep abreast of the most recent developments and modify your tactics accordingly. Have an open mind while trying out new marketing strategies, content types, and platforms.

10. Establish Connections with Influencers

By collaborating with influential people in your field, you can expand your audience and gain the trust of your intended audience. Find influencers who share your vision and collaborate with them to produce content that highlights your goods and services.

You may build a strong online presence that will support your business promotion, help you connect with your target audience, and help you reach your objectives by following these steps. Recall that creating a solid internet presence requires time and work, but the results are worth the investment.

Creating a Compelling Website: Your Online Home-Base for Information and Engagement

Operating a business, especially a physical one, without a website is becoming unfeasible. Customers use the internet for everything, including product research, business locations, and hours of operation. If you have things to sell, your website may help you reach new customers and grow your business quickly and affordably. Even a basic, well-designed website can provide you an advantage in your industry.

The ease of use of website design software has increased throughout time. Coding knowledge is not required to create a visually appealing and useful website. Whatever tool you use, there are a few basic guidelines and best practices to adhere to in order to present your business in the best possible light, make your website easy to use, and give it a polished appearance.

1. Ascertain the main objective of your website:

A business website can be used as a direct platform for e-commerce, allowing you to sell products online, or it can be used to provide basic information about your firm. The most crucial thing you need to do is clearly state what your firm does on the homepage, regardless of whether you design a straightforward website that informs visitors about what you do or a more intricate online buying experience. According to Erin Pheil, CEO of The MindFix Group, a website design firm formerly known as Followbright, clients shouldn't have to search far to find out if your business can meet their needs.

"Considerate your unique user experience and the path the user will take while browsing your website," advised Gabriel Shaoolian, Digital Silk's founder and CEO."Clients ought to have the option to rapidly achieve the centre target of your site, anything that the centre might be, and the actual reason ought to be built up as clients go all through your site."

You won't have to spend as much time setting it up if you don't intend to take payments through your website using Apple Pay. However, you'll need to employ an outside service to take your payments if you're a merchant or service provider and want to provide customers the choice to pay online. This will be discussed in greater detail later on in the article.

2. Select your domain name: One of the most important aspects of your website is your domain name. It's the URL you'll advertise on social media and share with both present and new customers. It should therefore be descriptive, simple to remember, and straightforward to type into a web browser. To prevent confusing customers, try to keep it brief and avoid using acronyms, numerals, and abbreviations.

Selecting your top-level domain (TLD) is another requirement. This is the last character (.com,. net, or.biz) that appears at the end of your domain name. Nontraditional TLD names, however, have been more popular recently. These TLDs might be based on the sort of business, like marketing, agency, or law, or on the geography, like nyc. The most popular option is still.com, even though these can be descriptive.

After deciding on a domain name, you must buy it from a domain registrar and verify that it is still available.

The following are a couple of notable space recorders.

- Domain.com
- Wix
- Square footage
- GoDaddy

Make sure you are not violating anybody else's protected name when you choose your new domain name by looking up copyrights. If your intended URL is already taken, you can either utilise a domain-buying service from a business like GoDaddy, which will contact the proprietors of your desired domain name, or you can phone the company using it and ask to buy it from them.

3. Select a web server.

Every website requires a host, or a server on which all of its content is kept permanently accessible to the general public. It's likely too costly for your small business to host your own website, so you'll need to choose an outside host.

Based on the financial constraints of your company, there are two options available to you. The less expensive option, a shared web host, entails sharing a server with other websites. Dedicated hosting, the second choice, is much more expensive but comes with your own private server and eliminates the need to compete with other websites that can slow down your website. A few website builders, including Squarespace and Wix, incorporate web hosting as part of their monthly plans.

Here are a few notable organisations that deal web facilitating administrations:

Ionos: Known for its cloud hosting services, this web hosting provider also provides other cloud-based solutions like servers and site backup. Plans and capacities differ.

A2 Hosting: A2 Hosting offers dedicated and shared hosting services.

DreamHost: DreamHost offers shared and virtual private server (VPS) hosting services in addition to plans specifically designed for WordPress hosting.

It's important to keep in mind that website hosting is by no means free for the hosting provider if you're searching for free hosting solutions. Therefore, in order to make up for the free hosting, they could use other strategies, such as putting banner advertising on your website.

According to Jim Cowie, co-founder of Deep Macro and former chief scientist at cloud-based internet performance startup Dyn, while selecting a host, take into account how well the vendor can respond to inquiries on its server locations and dependability.

"Can you show me how close you are to the major markets my customers will be in?" is an excellent question to ask. stated Cowie. "Measures of their performance should be visible to you from any reputable hosting provider."

As your company expands, you might discover that managing the traffic and operations of your website requires you to switch to a new web host or perhaps collaborate with several different ones. In order to ascertain your hosting requirements, Cowie suggested closely monitoring the functionality of your website and the user experience of your clients.

Develop your pages: A quality website consists of more than just a blank home page. You should make several pages with different sections of your business, such as a comprehensive catalogue of your goods or services or a blog area for corporate updates, using platforms like WordPress, Wix, or Squarespace. Regarding your website as a whole, make sure every page has a clear purpose, supports the main objective of the site, and has a call to action (CTA) that directs the user to another place, like "Learn More," "Sign Up," "Contact Us," or "Buy This."

One of the most important parts of a website is the contact page, which is your clients' primary point of contact. Make sure it has all the information your consumers need, including your company's phone number, email address, and, if applicable, physical location. In order to give your brand a human face, it's a good idea to include information about the founding team or staff on a "About" page.

Use a graphic designer or make one yourself if your company doesn't already have one for your website, business cards, and social media accounts. A unified brand image will make it easier for your customers to find your business online.

4. Make it clear what your company does: Reduce the scope of your company's operations to a single, succinct statement, and start there. It should be apparent to visitors what you do from the moment they appear on your homepage. Dozens of badly written pages are not as impactful as a few skillfully written ones.

Position the CTA wisely: CTA buttons work best when they complement the content on the page. On a product page, for instance, a "Buy Now" button would make sense; but, a "Contact Us to Learn More" button might be more suitable on the "About Us" page. Similar to this, a website with client testimonials may feature a button directing the visitor to your price and product offerings.

Automate increases in speed: Using internet resources, set up as many automatic speed increases as you can. Installing the appropriate plugins will cache certain elements of your website if you use a content management system, saving users from having to download anything more than once. Zalewski suggested WP Super Cache or W3 Total Cache for WordPress users, which compresses files and speeds up site navigation. If you're not very tech-savvy, you might need a web development partner for some of the more complex parts like caching and compressing files.

Steer clear of stock photos: The easiest way to take a fantastic website and make it mediocre is to use tacky stock photos. Using a snapshot of your team or office is the ideal option if you're looking for images to publish on your pages. Pheil continued, saying that excellent product photos boost revenue, so make an investment in outstanding images of the goods or services you offer.

5. Set up your payment system (if applicable): Businesses that wish to allow their consumers to make payments online must integrate electronic payment systems with their websites. However, not all business websites will need to follow this step. Using one of the top credit card processing services or e-commerce software is the simplest method to accomplish this.

Furthermore, a lot of web hosts integrate with e-commerce platforms or provide an internal shopping cart. Make sure the solution you choose is workable and adaptable enough to fulfill your demands both now and down the road by doing some study.

6. Test and publish your website: Verify that your website functions properly across all popular

browsers, including Microsoft Edge, Firefox, Safari, and Chrome, before declaring it live. Verify that images appear, links work properly, and the format is fluid by clicking on every page and feature on every browser. Although it will take some time, the work you do today will prevent future complaints from users who are unable to use specific functions.

Additionally, confirm that your website functions correctly on mobile devices, including tablets and smartphones. Given that Google and other search engines have switched to mobile-first indexing, which gives the performance of your website's mobile version priority when it comes to search engine results, you shouldn't skip this step.

Analytics is another crucial component that should be included from the start. Prior to the website's launch, you can resolve any problems and arrange for a suitable arrangement, according to Shaoolian. After the website goes live, you may track page performance and use analytics to ascertain why a certain page works well or poorly.

"To get some understanding into how your crowd is cooperating with your site, you can take a gander at which of your promoting efforts are showing the most noteworthy change rates and look at any [user] measurements, like city, program, and so on," Shaoolian exhorted. "You'll lose out on important data and be unable to determine which aspects of your website are successful or unsuccessful from the beginning if you... implement this [after] the site goes live."

Harnessing The Power of Social Media: Building Brand Awareness And Engaging With Customers

Social media has transformed communication, information sharing, and business practices, becoming an essential part of our everyday lives. It is an effective tool that small business owners may use to expand their consumer base, engage with clients, and expand their company.

We'll go over the advantages of social media for small company owners in this tutorial, along with some useful advice on how to use it to your advantage and accomplish your objectives.

Why Should Small Businesses Use Social Media?

Small businesses can use social media as a platform to connect with potential clients and increase brand awareness. In fact, a Hubspot study found that consumers are 71% more likely to make a purchase after seeing a recommendation on social media.

The following are some main advantages of social media use for small businesses:

Economical Advertising

Social media offers small businesses an affordable means of reaching a wide audience. Social media makes it possible to reach your target audience without going over budget, in contrast to more conventional marketing strategies like TV and print advertisements.

Updates, pictures, videos, and even live streaming are all free for businesses to share. This is a big benefit because traditional marketing strategies like print and television advertisements need large upfront financial outlays.

Enhanced Recognition of the Brand

You may expand the audience for your brand and make it more visible by setting up social media accounts for it. Creating interesting content is essential for gaining a devoted following and drawing in new clients. Companies may foster a closer relationship with their customers by using social media to communicate their brand story, values, and mission. This fosters a connection of trust and a long-lasting one with the clients.

Additionally, social media provides a number of tools including hashtags, mentions, and shares that can raise company awareness. Businesses can reach people beyond their immediate followers by utilising relevant hashtags. A brand's reach can also be increased through mentions and shares, since the material will be seen by the following of the individuals or businesses that make mention of it.

Enhanced Interaction with Customers

Social media gives you the chance to interact with your consumers in real time and gives businesses the chance to interact with their audience and create a community around their brand. Businesses may demonstrate to their clients that they appreciate them and are dedicated to giving them exceptional customer service by answering their messages and comments. Positive word-of-mouth advertising and referrals may result from this, raising brand awareness even further.

Additionally, you can conduct surveys and polls to allow clients to express their thoughts and offer insightful criticism. By doing so, companies will be able to better understand the wants and needs of their clients and adjust their products and services to better suit those demands.

Getting Useful Insights

Businesses can access a variety of data analytics tools on social media platforms that give them important insights on the behaviour, interests, and involvement of their customers. Businesses can obtain insights from the analysis of this data to assist them develop content that appeals to their target audience and more successful marketing campaigns.

The ability to track client participation is one of social media analytics' most important benefits. This includes indicators like likes, shares, and comments, which give businesses insightful information about how well their content is performing. Businesses can learn more about the material that appeals to their audience and modify their marketing strategy by keeping an eye on these data.

Advice on Leveraging Social Media's Power

Now that you are aware of social media's advantages for small businesses, follow these helpful pointers to fully utilise its potential:

Establish Your Objectives

Setting objectives is crucial before utilising social media. Are you trying to boost revenue, raise brand recognition, or cultivate a devoted clientele? After your objectives are clear, you can develop a social media plan that supports your company's aims.

Make sure your goals are time-bound, relevant, quantifiable, detailed, and feasible before setting them. Instead of stating that you want to "increase sales," for instance, make your objective to "increase sales by 10% in the next quarter through social media marketing." You may develop a more targeted and concentrated social media plan that fits your target audience and business objectives if you have certain goals in mind.

Select the Appropriate Channels

A key component of any effective social media marketing strategy is selecting the appropriate social media sites. The distinctive characteristics and user bases of various platforms can influence how successful your social media marketing is. When choosing which social media platforms to concentrate on, it's critical to take your target audience and company objectives into account in order to get the most out of your presence.

210

For instance, networks like TikTok and Snapchat might work better than Facebook or LinkedIn if you're trying to reach a younger audience. Consider using Pinterest or Instagram if you want to share visual stuff. Similarly, LinkedIn is an obvious choice if you want to build your professional network or position yourself as a thought leader. You may increase the effectiveness of your social media marketing campaigns and more effectively connect with your target market by being aware of the advantages and disadvantages of each platform and choosing the ones that are best for your company.

Make Interesting Content

Any successful social media marketing plan must include the creation of interesting content. Make sure your material is visually beautiful, useful, and relevant to your target audience if you want it to stand out from the competition. To keep your audience interested and involved, you can utilize a variety of content formats, including blogs, infographics, videos, and photos. But don't forget to maintain consistency in your brand language and make sure that the material you produce supports your company's goals.

Maintaining regular content posting is essential to keeping your audience interested. This communicates to your followers that you are engaged and committed to developing a relationship with them, in addition to keeping your brand at the forefront of their minds. It's also essential to reply to messages and comments right away to demonstrate to your followers that you appreciate their participation and input. You may develop a devoted following and raise brand awareness by producing high-quality content and communicating with your audience on a regular basis. These actions can eventually result in more conversions and sales.

Make use of Advertisement at Cost

To reach a larger audience and increase website traffic, consider using paid advertising on social media. You can increase the likelihood of conversion by creating ads that target particular demographics and interests through the use of social media platforms' targeting features.

Enhanced targeting, better visibility, and real-time outcome measurement are just a few advantages of paid social media advertising. You can broaden the audience for your company and connect with people outside of your present fan base by using sponsored advertising. Furthermore, you may maximise the return on your investment by limiting the population to which your adverts are seen by targeting particular demographics and interests. Lastly, a lot of statistics and tracking tools are available on social media platforms, so you can evaluate the success of your ads in real time and adjust your approach accordingly. Paid advertising can help you increase online visibility and generate more leads and conversions when combined with social media marketing.

Keep an Eye on your Analytics

You can monitor a number of indicators with social media analytics, including click-through rates, reach, engagement rates, and conversions. You may have a thorough insight of your audience's social media interactions with your brand thanks to these analytics. You may evaluate the effectiveness of your social media marketing initiatives and make data-driven decisions to strengthen your plan by examining these KPIs.

Social media analytics also let you monitor your progress toward your company objectives and assess the effectiveness of your marketing activities. With this data, you can make wise decisions to propel business growth, manage resources efficiently, and improve your campaigns in real time. You can maintain an advantage over competitors and create a more successful social media marketing plan by regularly reviewing your social media data.

It's evident that social media has a lot to offer small businesses, from increasing reach to enhancing client interaction. Nevertheless, social media success calls for much more than merely setting up profiles and sharing information. You may design a customised strategy that meets your target demographic and specific business objectives by putting the tactics covered in this guide into practice. In your social media endeavours, never forget to be persistent, imaginative, and patient while also making an attempt to add value for your fans. You can create a powerful social media presence that promotes sustained business success and growth if you put in the necessary time and effort.

Leveraging Digital Marketing Strategies: SED, PPC And Content Marketing for Growth

Digital Marketing: What Is It?

The utilisation of sites, applications, cell phones, web-based entertainment, web crawlers, and other computerised stages to advance and sell labour and products is known as computerised advertising. During the 1990s, as the web turned out to be all the more broadly utilised, advanced promoting started to acquire prevalence.

Computerised showcasing is every now and again seen as an additional device for organisations to arrive at clients and fathom their way of behaving, and it integrates a considerable lot of similar ideas as conventional promoting. Traditional and digital marketing strategies are frequently combined by businesses. In any case, web promoting has its own exceptional arrangement of challenges.

Via platforms like social media, mobile devices, and websites, digital marketing advertises goods and services.

There are a few strategies accessible to computerised advertisers to measure the outcome of their endeavours.

The capacity to hang out in a world brimming with computerised ads and different interruptions is one of the fundamental issues looked by computerised advertisers.

The Operation of Digital Marketing

To increase their market share and advertise their goods and services to prospective customers, businesses can employ a variety of marketing strategies and media. It takes a blend of deals, keenness and publicising skill to succeed. These responsibilities are handled by professional marketers, either in-house at specific businesses or outside at marketing agencies that might work with a wide range of clients.

Before, organisations depended entirely on print, radio, and TV for their showcasing endeavours. The internet gave businesses a new means to reach customers and gave rise to digital marketing, even though those alternatives are still available.

Companies were compelled to reconsider their marketing strategies and budgets in light of the emerging technologies and trends. In the early stages of digital marketing, email became a prominent medium for marketing. Subsequently, the emphasis switched to search engines like Netscape, which enabled companies to mark and keyword goods in order to gain visibility. The emergence of social media platforms such as Facebook allowed businesses to monitor user data and target very specific audiences with their messaging.

Nowadays, businesses may more easily promote their goods and services to customers wherever they may be thanks to smartphones and other portable electronics. According to a Pew Research Center research from 2022, 76% of American people have used smartphones to make internet transactions.

Channel Types for Digital Marketing

Since the 1990s, digital marketing channels have changed and are still changing. These are eight of the most widely used channels available right now.

Internet Promotion

Businesses frequently utilise their own website as the focal point of their online marketing campaigns. The most successful websites give a distinct and unforgettable image of the company, together with its goods and services. These days, a website has to load quickly, work well on mobile devices, and be simple to use.

Advertising Charged Per Click

Marketers can reach audiences on news and other websites and digital platforms by using pay-per-click (PPC) advertising. Advertisers can create PPC campaigns on Facebook, LinkedIn, X (previously Twitter), Google, Bing, Pinterest, and other platforms, and have their ads displayed to users who enter phrases associated with their goods or services.

Users can be divided up by these campaigns according to their geography, interests, or certain demographics (including age or gender). Facebook Ads and Google Ads are the most popular PPC services.

Marketing of Content

Reaching potential consumers with interesting written, visual, or video information is the aim of content marketing. After being posted on a website, the information is typically pushed via email marketing, social media, search engine optimization, and even pay-per-click advertising. Contrasted with publicising, content showcasing plans to be more downplayed, and the support's expected item or administration might possibly be unmistakably shown.

Email Promotion

Despite the misconception that emails are spam, email marketing remains one of the most successful digital marketing platforms. To get names for their email lists, many digital marketers utilise their other digital marketing channels. They then endeavour to change over those leads into clients through email promoting.

Marketing on Social Media

A social media marketing campaign's main objectives are to create trust and increase brand awareness. As you become more knowledgeable about virtual entertainment promoting, you might use it as an immediate showcasing or deals channel as well as to create leads. Two occasions of virtual entertainment showcasing are tweets and posts that are advanced.

Partner Promotion

One of the earliest kinds of advertising is partner showcasing, which has been revived by the web. In affiliate marketing, businesses and private "influencers" market the goods of another business in exchange for a commission each time a lead is generated or a sale is completed. Numerous well-known businesses, such as Amazon, offer affiliate programs that reward affiliates who assist in selling their products with millions of dollars.

Utilising Videos

Many internet users visit websites such as YouTube for relaxation, learning how-to videos, reviews, and before making a purchase. To direct a video promoting effort, advertisers can utilise any of various stages, like Facebook Recordings, Instagram, and TikTok. Organisations who join video with Website optimization, content advertising, and greater web-based entertainment promoting endeavours make the best progress with it.

Messaging via Text

Additionally, businesses employ text messages—also referred to as SMS, or short message service—to provide updates about their newest offerings and specials. Texting is another tool used by political candidates and nonprofit groups to advertise and raise money. Nowadays, a ton of showcasing drives empower clients to give or make an instalment with simply an instant message.

Digital marketing Key Performance Indicators (KPIs)

Key execution pointers, or KPIs, are utilised by both conventional and advanced advertisers. KPIs enable them to assess the long-term effectiveness of their marketing campaigns and evaluate how they stack up against those of their rivals.

Some of the most popular KPIs that marketers can use to assess their performance are as follows:

Rate of click-through: By calculating the percentage of individuals who clicked on a certain advertisement out of all those who may have seen it, this key performance indicator (KPI) is frequently used to assess the efficacy of internet advertising.

Conversion rate: This measure compares the proportion of individuals who completed a desired action, such as making a purchase, to the overall audience that a certain advertisement or promotion reached, and it goes significantly farther than the active visitor clicking percentage. Social media traffic measures the amount of users that engage with a business's social media pages, Likes, following, perspectives, shares, or potentially other quantifiable exercises are incorporated.

Website traffic is a measure of the number of individuals who visit a business's website over a specific amount of time. It can be used, among other things, to assist businesses in determining how well their marketing initiatives are bringing customers to their website.

Difficulties in Digital Marketing

For marketers, the digital environment presents unique obstacles. For example, advanced channels are becoming increasingly ordinary, and advertisers need to keep awake to date and figure out how to effectively utilise them. It can be difficult for marketers to evaluate and effectively utilise the vast amounts of data that these platforms enable them to collect.

Most importantly, it's getting more and harder to get customers to pay attention because they are constantly exposed to digital advertisements and other distractions.

In Digital Marketing, what is SEO?

The expression "website improvement" (Web optimization) alludes to various methodologies utilised by organisations to attempt to further develop site traffic and web index positioning. The likelihood that a customer will see a website and possibly click to visit it increases with its position on the search results page.

Utilising E-Commerce Platforms: Facilitating Online Sales and Reaching a Wider Audience

Any business's ability to succeed in the digital age of today is largely dependent on its online presence. And while owning a website is unquestionably important, there are other ways to connect with potential clients these days. Businesses today have a wealth of possibilities to explore and expand their reach beyond traditional bounds with the emergence of new internet sales channels.

Recognizing the Significance of Digital Sales Channels

The utilisation of online sales channels is crucial for optimising outreach and growing the clientele. Businesses may reach a wider range of demographics and improve their chances of closing deals by utilising a variety of channels. For example, selling goods on well-known e-commerce sites, social media platforms, and online marketplaces gives businesses access to a large number of prospective customers.

This broad reach promotes better relationships by facilitating customer engagement and raising brand visibility.

Using a variety of online sales channels also reduces the risk associated with relying too much on one platform and offers a safety net in the event of difficulties or changes. Long-term growth and profitability can be achieved by carefully considering various internet sales channels and allocating time and money to investigate them.

Frequently Used Internet Sales Channels

    a. Platforms for E-Commerce

E-commerce platforms are a crucial component of online sales channels since they give companies an easy-to-use, expandable means of connecting with clients. These platforms serve as online showrooms for businesses, enabling them to showcase and sell their goods and services. They provide services including inventory management, customer data analysis, and secure checkout systems.

For instance, companies can quickly and simply establish an online store, alter the design, and effectively handle orders by utilising e-commerce systems.

Furthermore, a lot of e-commerce platforms come with integrated marketing tools and are integrated with well-known payment gateways, which facilitates customer acquisition and transaction processing. One example of this is Amazon.

One of the most well-known online retailers is Amazon. It offers a vast audience of prospective clients, which makes it an advantageous platform for companies. Sellers gain from Amazon's extensive market reach and reliable brand, which may result in higher sales. Sellers can access Amazon's efficient order fulfilment and customer care skills by leveraging its strong infrastructure.

Amazon also provides advertising options to increase product visibility and increase sales. To differentiate your product listing from the competition, make sure it has both high-quality photos and pertinent keywords. Building trust and influencing purchase decisions can also be achieved by utilising Amazon's customer reviews and ratings.

b. eBay

eBay is a well-liked online sales platform that provides companies with a large audience. Sellers can access a worldwide customer base because of its vast user base. The platform gives businesses flexibility in their selling tactics by supporting both fixed-price and auction-style listings. Additionally, eBay offers features and tools for listing optimization, like thorough product descriptions and excellent photos.

The site also provides buyer protection policies, which can boost customers' confidence and trust when making purchases. Businesses can increase their online exposure and sales potential by taking advantage of eBay's large audience and sophisticated selling tools.

c. Shopify

The well-known e-commerce platform Shopify is a flexible online sales channel that provides several advantages for companies. The following justifies its consideration:

Simple setup: Setting up a Shopify store doesn't require technical knowledge thanks to its user-friendly interface.

Personalization choices: Design the store with your brand in mind to provide customers a flawless shopping experience.

Integrations with apps: Shopify offers a wide range of apps to increase functionality, ranging from inventory management to marketing tools.

Shopify makes sure your store is optimised for mobile devices so it can meet the needs of the increasing number of consumers using smartphones.

Options for payment gateways: Provide clients with convenience by accepting payments from several suppliers seamlessly.

Optimization for search engines: Built-in features increase your store's organic traffic by increasing its search engine presence.

With Shopify, companies can create a polished and profitable online presence without having to deal with the hassles of starting from scratch with website development.

Platforms for Social Media

For optimising reach, social media sites provide useful online sales channels. These platforms offer a large audience base to target potential clients, with billions of active users. Businesses may display and sell their products straight within the social media interface with tools like Facebook Marketplace and Instagram Shopping.

Furthermore, buyable pins on websites like Pinterest enable users to make purchases, increasing the potential for revenue. Businesses may reach a large user base on social media, interact with consumers through tailored advertisements, and eventually increase revenue by utilising these platforms. For increased visibility and conversions, it's critical to optimise product descriptions, photos, and social media marketing.

a. Marketplace on Facebook

Facebook Marketplace is a well-liked online sales platform that gives companies access to a sizable pool of prospective clients. It makes it possible for people and companies to sell both new and used goods straight on the Facebook network. Facebook Marketplace, which has millions of active users, gives businesses a space to display their goods and get in touch with potential customers.

The audience that Facebook Marketplace already has is one benefit of using it. Businesses may reach the current user base and improve their chances of making sales by selling products on the Marketplace. Moreover, sellers can easily interact with prospective customers, respond to questions, and finalise deals thanks to the platform's connectivity with Facebook Messenger.

Facebook Marketplace also permits customised advertising. Companies can leverage Facebook's vast user base to craft highly targeted advertising campaigns that precisely target the target market. Businesses may make sure that people who are most likely to be interested in their products see them by leveraging features like interest-based targeting and location targeting.

b. Purchasing on Instagram

Businesses hoping to expand their customer base might find an efficient online sales channel with Instagram Shopping. Here are some important things to think about:

Appeal to the Eyes: Use Instagram's visually stimulating platform to highlight your products with stunning photos or videos.

Shoppable Tags: To make it easier for customers to find and buy your products, use the tagging tool on your Instagram photos to include product details and links.

Customer Engagement: Promote user contact by quickly answering questions, comments, and direct messaging. Interact with prospective clients to increase conversions and foster trust.

Influencer Collaborations: Use the posts and tales of relevant influencers who share the same values as your company to market your goods. Sales and a wider audience may result from this.

Recall that having a vibrant and eye-catching Instagram presence can greatly increase the likelihood of making transactions online.

c. Buyable Pins on Pinterest

Pinterest Businesses may easily sell their goods directly on the site with Buyable Pins. Users may browse and buy things without ever leaving Pinterest thanks to Buyable Pins. Potential clients will find online buying easier and more convenient with the help of this functionality, which streamlines the process. Businesses can reach a larger audience by leveraging Pinterest's vast user base through the usage of Buyable Pins.

For companies in sectors where visual appeal is important in driving sales, like fashion, crafts, and home décor, this internet sales channel is especially helpful.

Internet Auctions

Online marketplaces are well-known venues for online sales where a variety of goods from many vendors can be found in one location. These platforms give users an easy way to shop while giving sellers access to a huge user base. Through the utilisation of online marketplaces, companies may capitalise on pre-existing customer confidence and brand awareness, expanding their reach without requiring intensive promotional endeavors.

Online marketplaces that serve a variety of product categories and target consumers include Etsy, Alibaba, and Walmart Marketplace. By using these marketplaces, companies can grow their customer base, boost revenue, and get recognition in their niche markets.

a. Etsy

Etsy is a well-known online marketplace that specialises in selling vintage and handcrafted goods. It offers a forum for innovative companies to exhibit their one-of-a-kind items to millions of active buyers. For vendors trying to reach a certain market, the site's intuitive layout and integrated community make it a desirable choice. In addition, Etsy provides tools for promotions and configurable shop settings to assist merchants maximise their online visibility.

Businesses may reach a wider audience in the handmade and vintage market and access a highly engaged client base by using Etsy as an online sales channel.

b. Alibaba

Alibaba is one online sales platform that provides firms with a lot of chances to access a worldwide audience. Alibaba is a well-known B2B marketplace that brings together international buyers and sellers, making it the perfect venue for importing and exporting commodities. Businesses can reach new markets and grow their clientele thanks to its wide reach and variety of product categories.

Companies can connect with potential customers, exhibit their products, and use Alibaba's tools for efficient communication and negotiation by creating a profile on the platform. Increased sales and business expansion may arise from this, particularly for companies that cater to a global clientele.

d. The Marketplace at Walmart

Walmart Marketplace provides businesses with an extensive online sales channel to connect with a diverse clientele. The platform offers sellers the chance to expand their consumer base and boost sales thanks to its wide range of product categories and vast customer base. Businesses may take advantage of the confidence and trust that come with the Walmart brand by listing products on Walmart Marketplace.

In addition, the marketplace offers resources and tools for enhancing product listings, drawing clients with advertising campaigns, and examining performance indicators. To stand out in the crowded marketplace, merchants must provide competitive pricing, excellent product photos, and captivating product descriptions because competition can be fierce.

CHAPTER 6

Marketing and Sales Mastery: The Art of connecting With Customers

The lifeblood of any firm is its sales. Whether you're selling products, services, or even ideas, having strong sales skills is crucial. It should come as no surprise that sales knowledge has been in-demand, as evidenced by the growth of colleges designed to hone these skills. The curriculum known as the "Ultimate Sales Mastery Program" has garnered significant notice. We'll examine what makes this program unique, why it matters in the cutthroat market of today, and how it can enable individuals to have amazing success in sales.

Comprehending the Sales Mastery

The Ultimate Sales Mastery Program is a thorough training course designed to help individuals become exceptional salespeople. It's not just about perfecting sales techniques; it's also about developing a winning mindset and giving participants a broad range of skills to effectively navigate the challenging world of sales.

1. Mastery of Mindset

The core of the program is attitude mastery. The psychological toll that rejection and setbacks can have on a salesperson is well known. Developing resilience, confidence, and a growth mentality is emphasised heavily in the Ultimate Sales Mastery Program. Participants gain the ability to view failures as opportunities for growth and to accept rejection as a necessary step on the path to success. Top-performing salesmen can be distinguished from the competition by their mental toughness.

2. Strategies and Techniques for Sales

Naturally, sales depend on having a solid grasp of the art of persuasion, and this course covers a wide range of sales techniques. Participants gain the abilities necessary to successfully complete deals, from creating compelling sales pitches to comprehending the psychology of buyers. Participants are assisted in applying these tactics in a real-world scenario through role-playing exercises and simulations.

3. Skillful Interaction

In sales, communication is crucial, and the curriculum places a lot of emphasis on honing this skill. In order to interact with a variety of customers, participants learn how to actively listen, pose insightful questions, and alter their communication style. Good communication is beneficial for closing deals as well as building enduring connections with customers.

4. Building Trust and Relationships

In the modern market, trust is a precious commodity. The Ultimate Sales Mastery Program shows participants how to build trust with customers by being truthful, forthcoming, and committed to offering value. Developing strong relationships with clients encourages recommendations and repeat business, both of which are important drivers of increased sales.

5. Sales Driven by Data and Technology

Salespeople need to make the most of technology and data since the world is becoming more digital. The most latest tools and technologies used in sales are covered in the training, including data analytics and customer relationship management (CRM) systems. Participants will gain knowledge on how to effectively evaluate their sales performance, target the right customers, and make informed decisions using data.

6. Productivity and Time Management

Since time is a scarce resource in sales, the curriculum includes training on efficiency and time management. Learners get skills in setting goals, prioritising tasks, and increasing productivity. These skills help salespeople stay focused and organised so they can concentrate on what really matters—completing transactions.

7. Getting Past Objections

Participant strategies for handling objections are given throughout the training, as they are a normal aspect of the sales process. Through role-playing and case studies, participants learn how to overcome common objections and turn them into opportunities to showcase the value of their products or services.

8. Compliance and Ethics in Sales

Sales ethics are crucial, and the training emphasises how important these ethics are. By learning about industry norms and ethical guidelines, participants may make sure they carry out their sales activities honourably and legally.

Understanding Customers Psychology: Identifying Needs, Motivations and Buying Behaviour

It's critical for marketers and business owners to comprehend the psychology of consumer purchasing behaviour. You may increase your chances of success and customise your marketing efforts by knowing why and how consumers make judgments about what to buy.

What Is Purchase Behavior of Consumers?

Consumer purchasing behaviour is the study of how and why people make purchases of products and services. Businesses must have a thorough understanding of consumer behaviour in order to develop marketing plans that effectively attract new clients and boost sales.

Numerous elements, including psychological, cultural, societal, and economic ones, have an impact on consumer behaviour. Depending on the person, their background, and their environment, these variables might differ substantially. Additionally, you may use behavioural segmentation—a technique that further customises each client touchpoint—to separate these customers based on their behaviour.

Affecting Factors of Consumer Behaviour

1. Individual Variables

Individual characteristics are major determinants of the various buyer kinds. These variables include things like personality, lifestyle, gender, age, and income.

Age: Needs and preferences vary among different age groups. While older consumers would favour durability and usefulness, younger consumers might prioritise the newest fashion trends and technology.

Income: Consumers with higher incomes might have more purchasing power and be prepared to pay a premium for superior goods and services. Conversely, customers with lower incomes might place a higher value on affordability and show greater sensitivity to pricing.

Gender: When it comes to goods and services, men and women could have distinct tastes. Men might be more interested in technology and athletics, for instance, whereas women might be more drawn to fashion and beauty.

Lifestyle: A customer's complex purchasing behaviour may be influenced by their lifestyle. An active person, for instance, might be more interested in fitness-related goods and services. On the other hand, a person who places a higher value on relaxation might be more drawn to opulent travel and spa services.

Personality: The characteristics of a customer's personality can influence their purchasing behaviour. Extroverts, for instance, can be more drawn to social gatherings and events, whereas introverts would prefer solitary pursuits like reading and watching movies.

These individual characteristics may have an impact on a consumer's purchasing decisions and habits. Because of this, companies ought to take these things into account when formulating marketing plans and designing goods and services that appeal to their target market.

2. Aspects of Psychology

The influence of psychological elements on consumer behaviour is significant. These elements, which primarily concern how consumers perceive, understand, and process information about a consumer transaction, are internal and subjective.

A few of the major psychological elements influencing consumer behaviour are perception, learning, motivation, beliefs, and attitudes.

The internal drive or desire that propels customers to take an action, such as making a purchase, is referred to as motivation. Motivation can be influenced by a number of things, such as objectives, needs, and wants on an individual basis.

A customer driven by the desire for security, for instance, could be more inclined to invest in safe financial products or buy insurance.

The term "perception" describes how customers understand and interpret details about a good or service. Perception can be influenced by a number of things, such as the consumer's expectations, cultural background, and prior experiences.

A customer who has encountered a brand positively, for instance, might have a more positive opinion of that brand than a customer who has never encountered the brand.

Learning is the process by which customers pick up new information, abilities, or perspectives regarding a good or service. A variety of methods, such as conversation, observation, and firsthand experience, can be used to learn. A customer's belief about a product or service refers to their cognitive framework or presumptions about it. For instance, a satisfied customer may be inclined to buy the same product again. Beliefs may stem from social influence, cultural ideals, or personal experience. For instance, people are more likely to buy organic foods if they think they are healthier.

A consumer's attitude is their overall assessment or understanding of a good or service. Positive, negative, and neutral attitudes can all be influenced by a variety of things, such as marketing messaging, social influence, and one's own experiences.

For instance, a customer who has a favourable opinion of a brand is more likely to tell others about it or make another purchase from it.

By comprehending these psychological elements and how they affect customer behaviour, companies may create marketing campaigns that successfully appeal to their target market. Businesses can enhance customer relationships and increase revenue by catering to the motives, perceptions, beliefs, and attitudes of their clientele.

3. Social Elements

Consumer behaviour is heavily shaped by social variables. The following are significant social variables that affect purchasing decisions:

A group or society's shared ideals, practices, habits, and artefacts are referred to as its culture. Consumer behaviour is shaped by culture in three ways: it affects what people purchase, how they buy it, and why they buy it. For instance, haggling over pricing is common in certain cultures whereas fixed prices are the standard in others.

Family: Members of the same family have a big say in what each other buys. Wives frequently make joint purchasing decisions, and kids frequently have an influence on what their parents buy. Family roles and dynamics also come into play, such as who gets to make the final decision on what to buy.

Reference teams: An individual looks to a reference group of people for advice on behaviours, values, and social norms. Reference groups may consist of close friends, relatives, coworkers, or public figures. Individuals' purchasing decisions may be influenced by the beliefs and behaviors of certain groups.

Class and society:

People who belong to the same social class have comparable incomes, levels of education, occupations, and lifestyles. Consumer behaviour can be influenced by social class in a number of ways, including where consumers shop, what things they buy, and how they decide what to buy.

Businesses can create marketing strategies that resonate with their target demographic by taking these social elements into consideration. A company catering to the upper class would, for instance, wish to position its products as exclusive or high-end, whilst a company aiming for a younger market might want to concentrate on influencer and social media marketing.

4. Contextual Elements

Situational factors are outside circumstances, such as the time, place, and occasion of the purchase, that influence customer behaviour. These elements, which include the following, may affect a customer's choice of what to buy:

One contextual element that may have an effect on customer behaviour is time. The time of day, day of the week, and season of year are examples of situational aspects associated with time. For instance, people might be more likely to buy holiday-themed goods during the relevant holiday season or ice cream throughout the summer.

Location: The place of purchase has the potential to impact the actions of customers. For example, people could be more inclined to buy expensive goods at posh department stores or malls.

Purchasing Occasion: Purchase occasions have an effect on customer behaviour as well. A buying occasion could be a unique occasion, such a wedding or Valentine's Day, that prompts a purchase.

Situational circumstances have the potential to greatly influence customer behaviour and present firms with chances to customise their marketing plans to fit particular scenarios or events. For instance, in order to take advantage of the spike in consumer spending during the Christmas season, a retailer can provide discounts or promotions with a seasonal theme.

Developing Customer Personas: Creating Detailed Profiles of Your Ideal Customers

Who are the personas of your customers?

Customer personas are made-up or partially made-up characters that are meant to evoke and represent a specific kind of customer. These helpful reference points and insight tools, often referred to as buyer personas, user personas, and marketing personas, are beneficial for a range of sales, marketing, and communication initiatives.

Customer personas can be used to better focus marketing communications to the specific needs of a group or individual by segmenting audiences and improving messaging. When implemented correctly, customer personas can improve lead generation, customer happiness, and conversion rates by helping marketers better understand their target market.

Customer personas consist of multiple attributes that are derived from comprehensive audience insights, including market research, website analytics, and direct customer input. This could include their age, occupation, level of education, location, interests and hobbies, obstacles they encounter, goals and aspirations, attitudes and views, and so on. It includes pretty much any criterion that sheds light on consumers' emotions so that advertisers can better engage them.

Through research, surveys, and interviews with a variety of clients, prospects, and people outside of your contact network who might be in line with your target market, buyer personas can be developed.

These are some useful techniques for obtaining the data required to create personas.

1. Examine your contacts database to detect patterns about the ways in which specific leads or consumers find and interact with your content.

If you are developing forms for your website, make sure that form fields gather pertinent information about your persona. If the company size is a determining factor for all of your personas, for instance, ask each lead on your forms about the size of their organisation.

Think about what your sales staff has to say about the leads they are interacting with the most. What assumptions may they make about the various clientele that you cater to the most effectively?

Find out what aspects of your product or service customers and prospects find appealing by conducting interviews.

What makes buyer personas crucial for your company?

- Product development is informed by buyer personas.
- Researching your target consumer in-depth isn't just for marketing purposes. These are valuable insights to include in your product development process during the research and development stage.
- Gaining insight into the daily experiences of your ideal client will help you come up with creative ways to enhance your offering.

For instance, let's say you own a kitchen equipment firm and your buyer persona study indicates that your ideal client is from the South, where grilling is popular all year round. This could be a chance to create and market grilling tools or enhance current kitchen tools to make them more suitable for use in both indoor and outdoor cooking settings.

2. Lead nurturing, demand creation, and lead generation material may all be optimised with the help of buyer personas.

Are you aware whether your ideal customer responds better to texts than to emails? Investigating buyer personas is one method of learning. Your demand generation tactics can be influenced by knowing the preferred communication channel of your prospective client.

Your target group may be more receptive to an SMS lead nurturing campaign than an email one if they prefer SMS communication. On the other hand, the information you find for your buyer personas might allow you to defend making whole website adjustments.

3. Buyer personas help you craft product marketing that speaks directly to your target market.

You may better understand your current and potential clients by using buyer personas. This facilitates the process of customising your messaging, content, services, and product creation to your target audience's unique wants, preferences, and issues.

For instance, you might be aware that your target customers are carers, but what kind of care do they often offer? What kind of background does your target consumer typically have? Creating thorough personas for your company is essential if you want to know exactly what drives your greatest clients.

Based on market research and insights obtained from your real consumer base (by surveys, interviews, etc.), your strongest buyer personas are created.

You may have as few as one or two identities or as many as ten or twenty, depending on your type of business. Start modest, nevertheless, if you're new to personas. If you need extra personalities later on, you can easily create more later.

This could include, for instance, experts who are too experienced for your business or product, students who are merely using your content for informational purposes, or prospective clients who are simply too costly to work with.

Due to a low average sale price, their tendency to churn, or their unlikeliness to make another purchase from your business, the potential clients can be too pricey. This information is useful because it enables you to focus your strategic execution so that your contributions directly impact your outcomes.

Crafting Compelling Marketing Messages: Resonating with Your Target Audience's Interests

For good reason, stories have been an integral part of human society for thousands of years. They evoke strong feelings in us, pique our curiosity, and make an enduring impression.

1. Recognizing who your target market is

One of the most important steps in creating a tale that appeals to your target audience is "understanding them." Learning about the people you're attempting to reach, their values, their interests, and their motivations are all part of it. You may use this information to craft a story that speaks to their experiences and suits their tastes.

For instance, you can decide to set your novel in a well-known urban setting and include relatable people if young adults are your target audience. You may choose to emphasize themes of nostalgia and family if you're aiming to appeal to an older audience.

You may write a tale that your target audience will connect with and appreciate more skillfully if you have a deeper understanding of them. Consider carrying out market research, polling your target market, or analyzing demographic information to learn more about your audience. You can write a tale that genuinely connects with your target audience if you take the time and make the effort to understand them.

2. Creating a distinct theme

Another crucial component of telling a story that appeals to your target audience is "developing a clear theme". In essence, a theme is the central idea or message that your narrative explores. It's what elevates your story above being a mere assemblage of incidents and personalities to the status of a well-crafted narrative that makes a significant statement about the world.

It's crucial to consider what you want your tale to communicate as well as what your intended audience would find interesting and pertinent when coming up with a theme. Your theme should be relevant to your audience and relate to their goals, values, and life experiences.

If working women are your target audience, for instance, you could write about topics like managing the rigors of motherhood, striking a balance between work and family, or following one's dreams in the face of setbacks. You may choose to concentrate on themes of friendship, self-discovery, or figuring out one's place in the world if young people are your intended audience.

You may write a story that not only interests and amuses your readers, but also connects with them on a deeper level by creating a distinct theme. When a tale hits home for them on that level, it becomes a part of them long after they've put the book or movie down.

3. Developing personalities that are relatable

A key to writing a story that connects with your intended audience is "creating relatable characters". A story's characters are its heart and soul, and drawing the audience in and holding their attention requires developing relatable characters.

Characters who the viewer can relate to on a personal level are considered relatable. They might relate to the audience in terms of problems, goals, or experiences. A relatable character increases the likelihood that the audience will be interested in the plot and care about the character's outcome.

Characters should be complex and multifaceted rather than one-dimensional caricatures in order to

263

be relatable. Make sure they are human, with both strengths and faults, by taking into account their histories, motives, fears, and hopes.

Making your characters relevant to your target audience in particular is also beneficial. This could entail imbuing the character's personality and background with aspects of the target audience's culture, experiences, or hobbies.

You may establish a relationship with your audience and make sure that your story speaks to them personally by making your characters likeable. Furthermore, viewers are more likely to be engrossed in the narrative and attentive from start to finish when they have a connection to the characters.

4. Increasing hostility and confrontation

"Building tension and conflict" is a crucial part of telling an engaging story to your audience. The plot advances, the audience is kept interested, and a sense of urgency and suspense are created by tension and conflict.

In a story, conflict can take many different forms, ranging from internal problems within a single character to exterior confrontations between characters. A feeling of unease or worry is produced by tension, which can be increased in a number of ways, including by introducing challenges for the characters to face, suspenseful scenes, and foreshadowing.

Finding a balance is crucial while escalating tension and conflict. The plot may feel overwhelming or unrelatable if there is too much conflict and stress, and it may seem dull and uninteresting if there is not enough. It's critical to strike the right balance between intensity and engagement to keep viewers interested.

Furthermore, there should be a connection between the theme and the characters and the struggle and tension. It should flow organically from their aspirations, experiences, and motives in order to forward the plot and make the theme come to life.

You may write a captivating, suspenseful narrative that keeps readers interested and involved in the plot by adding tension and conflict to your story. Furthermore, when viewers are engaged, they are more likely to recall the narrative and be affected by it even after they have stopped viewing or reading it.

5. Acting rather than narrating

A writing tenet known as "showing, not telling" suggests that instead of only telling the audience what is happening, you should allow them to experience the story via the characters and events. It's a method of keeping the audience interested and letting them come to their own conclusions as opposed to spoon-feeding them facts.

It works better to describe a character's body language, voice tone, or the circumstances leading up to their melancholy rather than just expressing "the character was sad" when you want to convey that they are depressed. A stronger bond and greater memorability are formed when the audience is able to share in the story through the characters and events.

Another strategy to keep the audience interested and let them utilise their imagination is to show rather than tell. The audience is able to experience the story more fully and becomes more immersed in it when they arc required to fill in the details.

Think about how you may write rich, sensory descriptions that let the reader experience the story through the characters and events in order to use the showing, not telling, approach in your writing. Let the viewers learn things through the narrative; do not impose your own explanations on them.

You may convey a tale that connects with your audience and enables them to experience it more deeply by using visuals rather than words.

6. Using conversation to move the plot forward

"Using dialogue to advance the story" is one of the most effective strategies writers can use to keep readers interested and make sure they grasp the plot. Characters can communicate with one another through dialogue, which also allows them to convey their feelings and thoughts and disclose important plot details.

Keep the language convincing and natural while using it to move the plot along. The dialogue between the characters should advance the plot and represent their goals, personalities, and experiences.

Furthermore, speech must divulge significant details about the narrative without being artificial or forced.

In order to create suspense and conflict, conversation can also be used to have characters quarrel or have arguments, which heightens the drama in the narrative. Conversely, conversation can also be employed to inject comedy, lighten the tone, or make the narrative funnier.

Generally speaking, conversation should be brief, snappy, and direct in order to move the plot along. Prolonged and meandering speeches have the potential to become monotonous and disinterest the listener. Instead, strive for clear, succinct speech that advances the plot and has a purpose.

You may write a more captivating and dynamic narrative that keeps your audience interested and involved by using dialogue to move the plot along. Furthermore, when viewers are engaged, they are more likely to recall the narrative and be affected by it even after they have stopped viewing or reading it.

7. Including feelings in

Writing a story that connects with your audience requires "incorporating emotions," which is a critical component. Stories become relatable, memorable, and powerful because of their emotions. You can establish a stronger bond and enable the audience to engage with the story on a deeper level by appealing to their emotions as well as those of your characters.

Make sure the feelings you choose to include in your story are true and true to yourself. The characters, their goals, and the story's events should naturally elicit the feelings. They should also convey the feelings that members of your target audience could feel in analogous circumstances. This will help to establish a link and increase the relatability of the narrative.

Achieving equilibrium is crucial while integrating emotions. A story that has too many emotions may come across as overpowering or unrelatable, while one that has too few emotions may come off as dull and uninteresting. Achieving the ideal balance is crucial to making the audience feel engaged in the narrative and able to relate to it.

Furthermore, it's critical to employ emotions to advance the plot and create tension and conflict. Characters' motivation might come from their emotions, which can also heighten the tension and sense of urgency. They can also assist the story's theme come to life and enhance its memorability.

You may make your tale more memorable and effective by adding emotions to it. This will allow your audience to connect with your story on a deeper level.

8. Creating a concise message

In order to write a story that appeals to your target audience, "establishing a clear message" is a crucial first step. Essentially, the story is attempting to convey to the audience a clear message. It might be a comment on the state of the world, a moral lesson, or a call to action. Whatever the lesson, it ought to be assiduously integrated into the narrative so that it appears to be an inherent and organic part of it.

Maintaining simplicity and concentration is key to crafting a clear message. A message that is too complicated or nuanced may be hard for the audience to comprehend and lessen the story's effect. Rather, try to convey a message that is clear-cut, understandable, and memorable.

Maintaining the message's relevance to the intended audience is also crucial. The message needs to resonate with the experiences, values, and worldviews of the listeners. The likelihood that the audience will relate to and remember a tale increases when they recognize themselves mirrored in it.

Furthermore, the message ought to align with the story's theme and tone. A message that is inconsistent with the tone or concept of the story may come across as forced or inappropriate, which lessens the story's overall impact.

You can make a tale that is more impactful and memorable for the audience by clearly stating your point. A narrative with a clear message can uplift, inform, or amuse the audience while also fostering a stronger bond between them and the outside world.

Selecting an engrossing environment

Writing a story that appeals to your target audience requires careful consideration of "choosing a compelling setting". The setting, or the place where the story is set, can have a significant impact on the tone, feel, and mood of the narrative.

The target audience should be taken into account while selecting a setting, as well as the kind of atmosphere that will appeal to and be most relevant to them. A story set in a small village, for instance, might be more relatable to a more conventional or rural audience, but a story set in a future city might appeal to a tech-savvy audience.

The setting should be used to further the tale in addition to being interesting and timely. A richly detailed and well-described location can assist the viewer feel a feeling of place and make the story come to life. A well-selected and skillfully employed location can also contribute to defining the tone, establishing the mood, and giving the story's actions context.

It's crucial to take the concepts and feelings you wish to portray in the story into account while selecting a setting. A bright and cheery atmosphere might be utilised to communicate a sense of hope and optimism, whilst a dark and ominous setting could be used to build tension.

You can write a story that feels rich and immersive and that engages the target audience on a deeper level by selecting a setting that is engaging. A compelling, captivating, and memorable story can be enhanced by a carefully selected location.

9. Visually communicating the tale Telling a story that connects with your target audience requires careful consideration. There are various ways to tell a story visually: through textual accounts of people, places, and events; through pictures; through films; and even through animations.

Because it increases audience engagement and produces a more vivid, unforgettable, and powerful experience, visual storytelling is crucial. The audience is more likely to become emotionally engaged with the story and become immersed in the characters and events when they can watch the drama play out in front of them.

When telling the tale visually, it's critical to be specific, sensory, and descriptive in order to paint a clear picture for the audience. You may, for instance, describe the sound of rustling leaves, the sensation of moss beneath your feet, and the scent of moist earth if the story is set in a pitch-black, scary forest.

In addition, visual storytelling should also be employed to improve the atmosphere, tone, and theme of the story. For instance, in a dark and scary thriller, you may describe menacing shadows, flickering lights, and the sound of footsteps reverberating through the shadows to evoke a sense of tension and anxiety through visual storytelling.

By presenting the tale visually, you can create a more engaging and memorable experience for the viewer. Combining written descriptions with visual storytelling techniques can make a story come to life and enable the audience to relate to the characters, actions, and themes on a deeper and more meaningful level.

10. Practice telling the tale and making it better

The process of "rehearsing and refining the story" is crucial to telling a tale that appeals to your intended audience. This is the stage where you take the story that you've produced and polish it till it shines, making any necessary modifications and enhancements to guarantee that it's the best it can be.

Iteratively rehearsing and fine-tuning the story entails putting it to the test with an audience, adjusting the narrative in response to their comments, and repeating the process until you're satisfied that the story is connecting with your target audience.

It's critical to monitor audience reaction during tale rehearsing and refinement, and to make necessary adjustments based on their input. For instance, you might need to alter the story's speed or structure or add more context or background information if the audience is finding it difficult to follow the narrative.

Additionally, it's critical to improve the story's effective parts and make sure they remain constant throughout. For instance, you might want to concentrate on ensuring that the dialogue is used consistently throughout the story and that it continues to resonate with the intended audience if it is believable and interesting.

It can take a lot of time and effort to rehearse and refine the story, but the process is worthwhile since it's essential to crafting an impactful narrative that connects with your target audience. You may craft a tale that is impactful, memorable, and engaging that resonates with the target audience on a deeper level by practising and honing it.

11. Evaluating how well your audience connects with the story

In order to develop a tale that resonates with your target audience, "testing the story's resonance with your audience" is a crucial stage. This is where you take your crafted story and see if the folks for whom it was meant are responding to it.

There are several techniques to find out if your tale resonates with your audience, such as focus groups, online questionnaires, or even in-person readings or presentations. Getting input from the target audience on what's working well, what needs to be changed, and what the audience is emotionally engaging with is the aim of assessing the story's resonance.

It's crucial to be receptive to criticism when gauging the resonance of the story, especially if it contradicts your initial expectations. For instance, it's crucial to pay attention to what the audience is saying and adjust your work accordingly if they say they're having problems following the plot or that they don't feel an emotional connection to the characters.

It's crucial to keep in mind that determining the resonance of the story is a continuous process, and that you should continuously solicit feedback and modify the narrative in response to it. This makes it more likely that the target audience will find the tale compelling and relevant over time.

One of the most important steps in creating a tale that will resonate with your target audience is to test the story's resonance. You can write a tale that engages the audience more deeply and leaves a lasting impression by getting input from the audience and incorporating it into future revisions and enhancements.

Implementing Effective Sales Strategies: Converting Leads into Customers and Building Customer Loyalty

Knowing your consumers is one of the most crucial parts of running any business. It might be challenging to develop content, build products, or advertise your company in a way that appeals to them without this understanding.

It's crucial to identify consumer behaviour before we look at ways to understand your consumers. In marketing, consumer behaviour refers to the choices and behaviours consumers make when using or making purchases of items.

What does consumer behaviour entail?

Consumer behaviour with respect to a product encompasses all aspects, including the decision to purchase it first, how they use it, and whether or not they decide to buy it again in the future. A multitude of factors can impact the behaviour of consumers, including

- Personal: income, age, and gender

- Social: friends and family
- Religious and traditional practices are cultural.
- psychological: learning, motivation, and perception

In instance, consumer psychology is a crucial area of research in marketing since it enables companies to comprehend the rationale behind consumer behaviour.

The reasons why consumer behaviour matters to businesses

Businesses may make better decisions regarding their products and services by having a deeper understanding of consumer behaviour. Businesses can modify their products to more effectively meet the requirements and desires of their target market by learning why consumers buy particular products and how they use them.

Businesses may improve the effectiveness of their marketing and advertising campaigns and increase their ability to contact and influence potential customers by having a deeper understanding of consumer behaviour.

Chapter 7

Embracing Innovation and Adaptability: Thriving in a Dynamic World

To remain competitive and create a robust business model, companies must embrace innovation and adaptation in the fast-paced, constantly-evolving business environment of today. Enterprises that possess the ability to predict and adapt to shifts are the ones that not only endure but also prosper during unpredictable times. Here are five essential tactics that will help you create a more resilient model and adjust to change in order to successfully traverse this ever-changing business environment and secure the long-term survival of your enterprise.

1. Recognize industry changes: It's critical to constantly watch and recognize changes in your sector if you want to stay ahead of the curve. Keep a close eye on new trends, developments in

technology, and shifts in customer behaviour. This necessitates reading trade journals, going to conferences, and actively maintaining connections with business networks. You can position your company to benefit from new opportunities and minimise potential disruptions by getting ahead of the curve in identifying industry developments. To stay on the cutting edge of your field, maintain your curiosity, investigate novel concepts, and be willing to attempt new things.

2. Keep an eye on how your audience is using social media: In the digital age, social media platforms have developed into effective instruments for comprehending consumer behaviour and preferences. Through proactive observation of your target audience's social media interactions, you can learn a great deal about their requirements, preferences, and expectations. To learn about their concerns and goals, analyse data, have discussions, and administer surveys. Your innovation efforts will

be guided by this knowledge, which will assist you in creating goods and services that meet the changing needs of your clientele. Track brand and industry keyword mentions using social listening technologies to stay abreast of the newest attitudes and trends.

3. Employ creative staff: The first step in creating an innovative workplace culture is to select staff members who have a natural flair for creativity and problem-solving. Seek out applicants who have a history of bringing about change, thinking creatively, and taking measured risks. Examine candidates' adaptability, receptivity to new ideas, and readiness to question the existing quo during the hiring process. Encourage experimentation, teamwork, and cross-functional communication in the workplace. Encourage innovation among your staff members, provide them the freedom and resources they need to make their ideas a reality, and empower them to share their ideas. Building a group

of creative thinkers will help your company become more adaptive and continuously improve.

4. Assemble a consultant team: During periods of rapid transition, consulting outside experts can yield insightful advice. Think about assembling a group of industry professionals, opinion leaders, and experts in fields related to your company to serve as consultants. These consultants can provide new insights, point out areas of blindness, and provide tactical advice. You may overcome obstacles, spot fresh opportunities, and make well-informed decisions that foster creativity and adaptation by working with experts. Their varied experiences can give you a more comprehensive grasp of the shifting environment and help you keep one step ahead of the competition. Form strategic alliances with other companies or groups to take advantage of resources and expertise that may be shared for both parties' growth and flexibility.

5. Pay attention to what consumers have to say. Since customers are the lifeblood of every company, it is essential to pay attention to what they have to say in order to adjust to their changing needs. Put in place reliable methods for gathering input, including as focus groups, questionnaires, and customer satisfaction studies. Engage clients in conversation on social media by answering their questions and taking quick care of their issues. Discover trends and patterns in consumer data to get understanding of their expectations and preferences. You may prioritise your consumers' demands and spur innovation by making well-informed decisions based on active listening.

Cultivating a Culture of Innovation: Encouraging New Ideas and Embracing Change

Development has arisen as a basic consideration driving organisations forward in the cutting edge economy. The meeting room can possibly cultivate and drive advancement inside an association since it fills in as the essential centre point of navigation.

Embrace a Development Outlook:

To drive development, everything begins with developing a development outlook. Embrace the conviction that development isn't just imaginable yet critical for remaining ahead in a serious market. Perceive that disappointment is a basic piece of the advancement interaction and a chance for development and learning. Urge yourself as well as other people to embrace a positive, strong demeanour towards change and novel thoughts.

Cultivate a Culture of Inventiveness:

Advancement flourishes in a climate that supports imagination. Support different points of view and welcome thoughts from all levels of the association. Make spaces for conceptualizing and thought sharing, where people feel enabled to break new ground. Underscore the significance of trial and error and urge representatives to proceed with well balanced plans of action to encourage innovativeness and reveal pivotal arrangements.

Support Cooperation:

Development is seldom a performance try. Develop a cooperative meeting room culture where colleagues can transparently trade thoughts, challenge suppositions, and expand upon one another's bits of knowledge. Cultivate cross-practical joint effort by separating storehouses and empowering assorted groups to cooperate on imaginative undertakings. By utilising the aggregate knowledge and skill of your meeting room partners, you can drive development according to a multi-layered viewpoint.

Remain Informed and Embrace Arising Patterns:

To drive advancement, remaining informed about arising patterns and innovations that influence your industry is pivotal. Urge board individuals to take part in nonstop learning and investigation effectively. Apportion time for progressing instruction and expert improvement to guarantee that the meeting room is exceptional to recognize and use arising open doors.

Underline Client Centricity:

A careful comprehension of client needs and desires ought to constantly be the main impetus behind development. Urge the meeting room to focus on client driven thinking in all dynamic cycles. Cultivate a culture of compassion where board individuals effectively look for bits of knowledge from clients, pay attention to their criticism, and coordinate it into development drives. By adjusting advancement endeavours to client needs, you can make items and administrations that genuinely resound and drive hierarchical development.

Embrace Innovation and Advanced Change:

In the present computerised age, innovation is a strong empowering influence of development. Embrace computerised change and the open doors it presents. Urge the meeting room to investigate arising advancements, like man-made consciousness, blockchain, or information examination, and evaluate their true capacity for driving development inside your association. Remain light-footed and versatile, embracing innovation as an impetus for extraordinary change.

Show Others how its Done:

As meeting room pioneers, it is urgent to show others how it's done and exhibit a guarantee to development. Embrace a mentality of ceaseless improvement and support trial and error. Champion advancement drives, assign assets for innovative work, and make impetuses for imaginative reasoning. By establishing the vibe from the top, you move others to stick to this same pattern and release their imaginative potential.

Driving development in the meeting room is a groundbreaking excursion that requires embracing change, encouraging imagination, and supporting a cooperative culture. By taking on a development mentality, stressing client centricity, and remaining informed about arising patterns, we can open the maximum capacity of development for hierarchical development. Allow us to make meeting rooms that rouse, engage, and drive change, pushing our associations into a future loaded up with vast conceivable outcomes. Together, we can shape a more splendid, more creative tomorrow.

Responding to Market Trends and Shifts: Adapting Strategies and Pivoting When Necessary

Changing your business plan is essential in the dynamic market of today. Businesses must keep ahead of the curve since new trends, technology, and consumer preferences are appearing on a daily basis. Perceiving the Need to Change Your Business Technique

In the dynamic business environment of today, markets are changing quickly, customer preferences are changing, and technology is developing at a rate that has never been seen before. As a result, companies need to adjust to these developments or risk losing their advantage over rivals.

Causes of Shifts in Business Strategy

There are a Number of Reasons why a Company Might have to Change its Approach:

Modifications to the market: A change in the market environment could make an existing company plan outdated.

Technological developments: Traditional business models may be disrupted by new technologies, requiring companies to innovate and adapt.

Competitive pressures: Businesses may need to change their strategies in order to stay relevant due to increased competition.

Consumer preferences: Businesses may need to adjust their techniques in light of moving purchaser requests.

Importance of a Business Strategy Pivot A corporation can remain relevant in a market that is undergoing rapid change by implementing a business strategy pivot. Businesses can seize new possibilities, maintain their competitiveness, and expand by changing their approach. A business runs the risk of losing market share and becoming irrelevant if it doesn't pivot.

A pivot can also assist a business in better coordinating its strategy with its objectives and mission. Businesses may make sure they are focused on the correct priorities and objectives by reviewing their strategy and making the required adjustments.

Important Steps for Business Strategy Pivot: To remain competitive in the fast-paced business world of today, organisations need to be able to quickly adjust and pivot their strategy. This is particularly valid during crisis situations or abrupt shifts in the market.

The essential actions that companies should take to change their company strategy will be covered in this section.

Determining the Need for a Shift

Identifying the need for change is the first step towards repositioning your business plan. This can be the result of shifting consumer behaviour, new competitors joining the market, or shifting market conditions. The secret is to take initiative and not put off making changes until it is too late.

Doing a SWOT analysis is one technique to determine whether a pivot is necessary. This will assist you in determining the advantages, disadvantages, opportunities, and threats facing your business. You may decide what adjustments to make to your business plan in order to remain competitive by analysing this data.

Examining the Market and Rivals

Examining the market and your rivals is the next step after determining that a pivot is necessary. To keep ahead of the game, you must be aware of what is going on in your sector and what your rivals are doing.

You can find new trends, opportunities, and risks in your sector by conducting a market analysis. This will allow you to modify your company plan as necessary. Analyse the advantages and disadvantages of your rivals as well as their advertising and sales plans. This will assist you in determining areas in which you can set yourself apart and obtain an edge over competitors.

Evaluate the Business Concept

Reevaluating your company model is the next stage after analysing the market and your rivals. This could entail altering your target market, distribution networks, pricing approach, or goods and services.

It is advisable to contemplate the long-term viability of your present business model. This could entail looking for new business models or revenue streams that complement the objectives and competencies of your organisation.

Formulating a Novel Approach

Creating a new plan that incorporates the modifications you have noticed in the other processes is the last stage in pivoting your business strategy. A thorough action plan that specifies the precise actions you must take to put your new strategy into practice should be part of this.

Your new approach should be in line with the overarching objectives and core values of your business. Additionally, it must be adaptable enough to change with the needs of the market and customer behaviour.

It is imperative that you change your business approach; it is not a choice. It's critical to have adaptability and be ready to adjust as the market does. You can maintain an advantage over your rivals and expand your company by doing this. It's critical to assess your existing approach, pinpoint areas for development, and implement the required adjustments when pivoting.

Embracing Technology and Automation: Streamlining Processes and Enhancing Efficiency

Automation is becoming a more popular tool for businesses in today's fast-paced workplace to improve productivity, reduce administrative work, and boost operational efficiency. Businesses that use technology effectively can avoid errors, cut down on manual labour, and concentrate on more strategic projects.

1. Determining Manual work that Can Be Automated: Finding manual work that can be automated is the first step towards adopting automation. Examine your administrative procedures and identify time-consuming, repetitive tasks that can be automated using technology. Data entry, report writing, document management, scheduling, and other tasks may fall under this category. You can free up important time and resources for higher-value work by automating these chores.

2. Picking the Correct Automation Tools: After determining which jobs need to be automated, it's critical to choose the appropriate automation tools. Numerous software programs are available to do various administrative tasks. Look into and select

products that meet the demands of your company, have easy-to-use interfaces, and work well with current systems. The correct technologies can greatly increase efficiency in any area—workflow automation, task management, or document automation, for example.

3. Simplifying Data Management: Administrative procedures must be carried out efficiently, which requires effective data management. Data integration between various systems, data validation, and data entry can all be made more efficient with the aid of automation. Businesses may reduce errors, guarantee data correctness, and enhance overall data quality by automating data processes. This increases productivity, permits quicker decision-making, and minimizes manual involvement.

Workflow automation is a potent instrument that has the potential to completely transform administrative procedures. Workflow automation gives businesses the ability to establish and automate notifications, approvals, and sequential activities. It also minimises bottlenecks and human handoffs while ensuring uniform processes. Workflow automation helps companies allocate resources more effectively, communicate better, and finish tasks more quickly.

5. Improving Collaboration and Communication: Within administrative teams, automation can have a big impact on improving collaboration and communication. Project management software, collaboration platforms, and communication tools are examples of solutions that make it easier to share information, provide real-time updates, and work effectively with teams or departments of varied sizes. This promotes efficient teamwork, lessens email overload, and streamlines communication.

6. Constant Improvement and Adaptation: Adopting automation calls for ongoing adaptation and improvement; it is not a one-time procedure.

Evaluate and assess the efficiency of your automated procedures on a regular basis. To find areas that could use improvement, ask users and stakeholders for their opinions. To keep your administrative chores productive and in line with your company objectives, stay current on the newest automation trends and technology.

Types of Efficiency in Business

There are various forms of business efficiency, and each is essential for a certain part of operations:

Cost Efficiency, Time Efficiency, Operational Efficiency

Let's examine each of these differences and their implications for an organisation in more detail.

1. Effectiveness of Operations

Streamlining internal procedures and workflows is the main goal of operational efficiency. This can include everything from streamlining manufacturing cycles and automating monotonous work to boosting worker productivity and inventory control. Businesses may greatly increase their operational efficiency by finding bottlenecks and optimising operations.

2. Economy of Cost

The goal of cost efficiency is to reduce costs without sacrificing the calibre of the goods or services. Companies might accomplish this through introducing energy-saving procedures, negotiating better prices with suppliers, or acquiring reasonably priced technology.

In addition to increasing profitability, cost efficiency gives companies the flexibility to provide competitive pricing to clients, giving them a competitive advantage in the marketplace.

Leaders, decision-makers, and financial stakeholders frequently place the greatest emphasis on cost efficiency. It's crucial to comprehend how cost effectiveness relates to other types of corporate efficiency, nevertheless. Improving efficiency across the board for the company's operations can lead to cost efficiency.

3. Time Effectiveness

The goal of time efficiency is to finish jobs and projects as quickly as feasible without sacrificing quality. This sort of efficiency is particularly crucial in industries where fast delivery is a competitive advantage. Enhancing time efficiency can be achieved via staff training, using technology to automate time-consuming tasks, and managing projects effectively.

Continuously Learning and Evolving: Staying Ahead of the Curve in a Competitive Landscape

In order to be competitive in the growing digital corporate world, it's critical now more than ever to continuously learn new tactics and abilities. You may develop, adapt, and apply your knowledge to the ever-changing digital business landscape through continuous learning.

You will have a significant advantage over other professionals who might be happier with their existing knowledge if you stay ahead of the game by continually seeking out new knowledge.

Keeping Up in a Changing Environment

The business environment is always changing due to market trends, client demands, and technological improvements. Entrepreneurs may stay up to date on new developments in their sector, advances in technology, and changing demands from their customers by engaging in continuous learning. Entrepreneurs that keep ahead of the curve are better able to recognize possibilities, make well-informed judgments, and modify their approaches to deal with the dynamic business environment.

Improving Knowledge and Skill in Business

Entrepreneurs have the chance to improve and expand their business acumen and skill set through ongoing education. They can have a deeper comprehension of fundamental business concepts including operations, marketing, finance, and leadership as a result. Entrepreneurs who increase their knowledge base are better able to run their businesses, make well-informed decisions, and encourage innovation inside their companies.

Promoting Creativity and Innovation

Entrepreneurs that never stop learning are able to think creatively and innovatively, coming up with original solutions to problems. Through exposure to a variety of viewpoints, industry best practices, and fresh concepts, entrepreneurs can unleash their creative potential and foster innovation in their companies. Participating in networking events, attending workshops, and learning from various industries can stimulate new ideas and spur entrepreneurial growth.

Developing a Robust Professional Network

Entrepreneurs have the chance to network with like-minded people, business leaders, and possible mentors through ongoing learning. Attending workshops, conferences, and industry events enables business owners to grow their professional networks, share expertise, and acquire insightful advice from seasoned experts. The assistance, direction, and chances for collaboration that a robust network may offer are critical for the success of an entrepreneur.

Gaining Capabilities for Effective Leadership

In order to lead their teams and propel business expansion, entrepreneurs require excellent leadership abilities. Entrepreneurs can build their leadership skills through lifelong learning and personal growth. They can pick up efficient problem-solving, decision-making, delegating, and communication skills from workshops, seminars, and executive education courses. Gaining these abilities enables business owners to motivate their staff, create a happy workplace, and successfully guide their companies to success.

Changing with the Times and Triumphing Despite Setbacks

Entrepreneurship is rife with obstacles and disappointments. Entrepreneurs that pursue continuous learning are better able to overcome challenges and learn from their mistakes.

Entrepreneurs are able to recognize areas for improvement, learn from their failures, and adjust their strategy as needed by adopting a growth mindset and actively searching out new information. The capacity to adjust and absorb lessons from setbacks is essential for sustained success in entrepreneurship.

Chapter 8

The Indomitable Spirit of Resilience: Overcoming Challenges and Achieving Success

We frequently experience failures and challenges on life's road, which can demoralise and demoralise us. However, what really determines our success is our capacity to overcome these obstacles and carry on. Herein lies the role of resilience. We will examine resilience's strength and how it can eventually help us succeed by enabling us to overcome adversity.

1. Recognizing resilience

Resilience is the capacity to adjust to and bounce back from challenging or stressful circumstances. It is more important to face obstacles head-on and figure out how to go through them than it is to avoid them. People that are resilient have a growth attitude, which sees obstacles as chances for improvement.

2. Strengthening Resilience: Over time, resilience is a talent that can be honed and enhanced. Thinking positively is one method to develop resilience. This entails reinterpreting obstacles as chances for development and concentrating on finding answers rather than moping over them. Having a solid support network of mentors, family, and friends can also help to provide the essential motivation and direction when things get hard.

3. The Significance of Resilience in Surmounting Obstacles: Resilience is vital in surmounting obstacles. When faced with hardship, resilient people are more likely to remain optimistic, stay driven, and take initiative to solve problems. They think they can overcome hurdles and see failures as transient. They are able to persevere through

difficult circumstances and come out stronger on the other side thanks to this approach.

4. Resilience Stories: There are countless accounts throughout history of people who showed incredible fortitude in the face of hardship. These inspiring tales encourage us to embrace the power of resilience in our own lives. From successful business people who experienced numerous disappointments before making their breakthroughs to athletes who overcame injuries and setbacks to reach the peak of their professions.

Embracing Setbacks as Opportunities for Growth: Learning from Mistakes and Refining Strategies

In the world of business, failure is unavoidable and can offer managers and leaders priceless teaching moments. By embracing a mentality that celebrates and learns from failures, organisations may promote

312

innovation, accelerate growth, and develop a culture that welcomes change.

The Value of Accepting Failure

Innovation and adaptation are essential for success in a fast-paced, cutthroat commercial world. But not every novel concept or endeavour will be successful, and innovation is frequently fraught with risk. Organisations can foster a culture that encourages people to take chances and think creatively by accepting failure and viewing it as a chance to learn and develop.

Lessons Acquired via Mistakes

Organisations can enhance their decision-making processes and strategies by learning useful lessons from their failures about what works and what doesn't. Failure can teach us important lessons, some of which are as follows:

1. Finding knowledge and skill gaps: Organisations can use failure to determine which areas require further resources or training in order to thrive in the future.

2. Improving systems and processes: Determining the underlying reasons of failure can point to areas where operations can be streamlined, communication can be improved, or risk management techniques can be put into place more successfully.

3. Promoting creativity and innovation: Organisations can develop an innovative culture that promotes growth and continual improvement by rewarding staff members who take chances and try out new concepts.

Accepting Failure as a Springboard for Success

At some point in their lives, everyone experiences failure, which is an unavoidable aspect of being human. Failure is by no means a definitive term, even though it can appear overwhelming and demoralising.

Rather, it acts as a furnace for the development of toughness and power.

Failure develops wisdom, fortifies character, and spurs us on to greater achievements.

Accepting Failure as a Growth-Catalyst

Failing is a necessary part of both professional and personal development, albeit it frequently results in frustration and disappointment.

Everybody fails occasionally, but you have the option to allow that defeat to destroy your confidence or to turn it into a learning opportunity.

Failure should be seen as a motivator for growth rather than as a moment of failure.

This is demonstrated by the well-known tale of Thomas Edison's ceaseless pursuit of the light bulb invention. Edison was famous for saying, "I have not failed," after every failed experiment. Just now, I discovered 10,000 ineffective strategies.

His breakthrough achievement was ultimately the result of his unwavering determination and readiness to learn from every setback; the same is true for you.

"Achievement is the culmination of little actions taken consistently over time." — Collier Robert.

Maintaining Focus and Determination: Persevering Through Difficult Times

It frequently takes resilience, focus, and resolve to navigate the problems of life and business. Whether you're dealing with obstacles in your personal or professional life, or even global disasters, it can be difficult to keep motivated and on course. On the other hand, you can overcome challenges and accomplish your objectives by creating practical plans and adopting a growth mentality.

1. Clearly define and deconstruct your goals

Set measurable objectives that are consistent with your overarching vision. Divide highly ambitious objectives into smaller, more doable tasks to foster a sense of accomplishment and prevent feeling overburdened.

2. Imagine Your Success

See yourself accomplishing your objectives on a regular basis. This kind of mental visualisation might help you stay motivated and bolster your self-belief that you can succeed.

3. Adopt a Growth Perspective

Adopt a growth mentality, which holds that intelligence and skill can be acquired via hard work and persistence. Having this mentality will enable you to see obstacles as chances for development and learning.

4. Acquire Robust Time Management Techniques

Set priorities for your work and make a timetable that enables you to concentrate on the most crucial tasks. To increase your productivity, use time management strategies like to-do lists and time blocking.

5. Develop Your Ability to Refuse

Refrain from overcommitting. Saying no to requests that don't fit your priorities or fill up your schedule is a valuable skill. This will help you stay focused on the important things and prevent burnout.

6. Take Care of Yourself

Make your physical and emotional health your first priority. Get enough sleep, eat a balanced diet, and exercise on a regular basis. Incorporate stress-reduction methods that support resilience and mental clarity, such as yoga or meditation.

7. Seek Out Assistance from Others

Never hesitate to seek assistance when you need it. Be in the company of people who will support you and who can lend an ear, advise, and words of encouragement.

8. Honour Your Accomplishments

No matter how tiny, acknowledge and celebrate your victories. This will increase your motivation and reaffirm your belief in your own skills.

9. Take Advice from Errors

Consider failures as teaching moments. Examine what went wrong and determine what needs to be improved. Make use of this information to improve your strategy and steer clear of the same errors.

10. Keep an optimistic mindset

Maintain an optimistic outlook and concentrate on your chances of achievement. Remain in the company of positive people and refrain from thinking negative or self-deprecating ideas.

Recall that being focused and determined is a continuous process rather than an isolated incident. There will be ups and downs along the road, but you can overcome obstacles, accomplish your objectives, and lead a satisfying life by using practical tactics and developing a resilient mindset.

Cultivating a Support Network: Seeking Guidance and Mentorship from Experienced Entrepreneurs

Building a solid support network is essential for success as an entrepreneur, regardless of experience level. Your entrepreneurial ventures might greatly benefit from having seasoned people around you who can offer advice, mentoring, and support.

1. Determine Possible Mentors

Look for mentors who have worked in your field or accomplished achievement in fields related to your objectives. Seek out people who are prepared to impart their wisdom, offer helpful criticism, and lend a hand as you negotiate the difficulties of becoming an entrepreneur.

2. Establish Connections

To meet possible mentors, participate in online forums, join entrepreneurial communities, and attend industry events. Have deep discussions, show that you are passionate about your business, and say that you would like to be mentored.

3. Take a Strategic Approach with Mentors

Make sure you are clear about your expectations and goals when you approach a possible mentor. Describe your goals for the relationship and how they may help you advance. Show that you are willing to put in the work and that you are committed to learning.

4. Clearly State Your Expectations

Talk about the parameters of your mentorship relationship, such as meeting frequency, methods of contact, and expected feedback. Make sure that everyone is aware of the terms of the agreement.

5. Stay Receptive to Input

Mentors can offer insightful advice as well as helpful criticism. Even though it can be difficult to hear, be receptive to their opinions. Utilise their advice to pinpoint problem areas and hone your strategy.

7. Grow Your Circle of Advise

Don't confide in just one mentor. Look for a varied set of people who can offer a range of viewpoints and levels of competence. Create a network of mentors that can help you with different facets of your business endeavours.

8. Look for Advice Outside of Mentorship

Although mentors can offer invaluable assistance, don't be afraid to look for advice from other sources as well. Seek assistance and specific knowledge from industry experts, seasoned professionals, and business advisers.

Recall that building a solid support system is an investment in your development on both a personal and professional level. Seeking advice and mentoring from seasoned businesspeople can help you overcome obstacles, obtain insightful knowledge, and improve your chances of succeeding in your endeavours.

Celebrating Milestones and Recognizing Achievements: Fueling Motivation and Driving Success

Motivation is the engine that propels achievement in any industry. Comprehending the importance of motivation and its potential to drive team performance is imperative for managers. In addition to raising output and efficiency, motivation also raises employee engagement and satisfaction, which creates a happier workplace.

This section will examine the significance of motivation by delving into various viewpoints and offering comprehensive insights to assist you in igniting motivation among your team members.

Recognizing the Significance of Motivation in the Business World

1. Increasing Productivity: In order to increase productivity in enterprises, motivation is essential. Employee engagement and goal-achieving attention are more likely when they are motivated. This boosts productivity and efficiency, which eventually improves the team's performance as a whole. Take a sales team as an illustration. A driven sales manager can greatly increase the team's output by setting high goals and offering rewards for reaching them. The manager increases their motivation by fostering a feeling of purpose and excitement, which raises sales numbers.

2. Improving Engagement and Satisfaction among Workers: Motivated workers are not only more efficient but also happier in their jobs. People feel a sense of success and fulfilment when they are motivated, and this adds to their total job satisfaction. Furthermore, as motivated people are more likely to collaborate well and actively participate in team activities, motivation promotes

employee engagement. For example, a manager who acknowledges and values the work of their team members can raise their motivation levels, which in turn increases engagement and job satisfaction.

3. Fostering a Positive Work Environment: Workplace culture can be influenced by motivation. A group of driven individuals are more likely to create a welcoming environment where everyone feels appreciated and inspired. Higher levels of cooperation, teamwork, and innovation follow from this. A manager can foster a healthy work atmosphere and inspire people to achieve to the best of their abilities by, for instance, encouraging open communication and offering opportunities for growth and development.

4. Retaining Top Talent: Employee retention and motivation are intimately related. People are more likely to stick with an organisation if they are driven and happy with their employment. This lowers

attrition rates and aids in keeping the team's best players. A manager who recognizes the value of motivation may help retain talented staff by putting tactics like work-life balance initiatives, career development plans, and recognition programs into place.

5. Inspiring Innovation and Creativity: In the workplace, motivation can act as a spark for creativity and innovation. People that are driven are more inclined to think creatively, experiment with novel concepts, and take measured chances. This may result in creative fixes, enhanced procedures, and eventually a competitive edge. A manager can inspire enthusiasm in staff members and encourage them to think creatively and contribute to the expansion of the company by, for example, promoting brainstorming sessions and praising original ideas.

Determining the importance of motivation in the workplace is essential to achieving success. Managers can use motivation to drive success within their teams by increasing productivity, improving employee satisfaction and engagement, fostering a positive work environment, holding onto top talent, and encouraging creativity and innovation. In order to achieve long-term success, managers must prioritise motivation and put measures in place to ignite and nurture it.

CHAPTER 9

Leaving an Enduring Legacy: The Impact of Your Entrepreneurial Journey in business

Many business owners aspire to leave a legacy in the realm of entrepreneurship. Leaving a lasting impression on your industry, society, and even the world is an essential part of creating a legacy firm, which extends beyond just financial success. We invite an experienced business coach for entrepreneurs to share his ideas in order to shed light on this inspirational trip. We will examine the fundamental ideas and techniques in this extensive post to assist you in creating a company that will endure throughout time.

Important Lessons for Creating a Business Legacy Beyond Financial Gains: Beyond just being financially successful, creating a legacy firm entails

329

making a long-lasting contribution to your sector, neighbourhood, and global community.

Vision and Purpose: Leaders such as Elon Musk, who have a strong vision centred on good change, lay the groundwork for a legacy firm.

Sustainable Growth: Take a cue from Warren Buffett and put long-term tactics—like reinvesting profits and cultivating consumer loyalty—above short-term gains.

Robust Corporate Culture: A flourishing culture, akin to that of Google and IBM, entails respecting fundamental principles, allocating resources for staff training, and welcoming diversity.

Customer-Centric Approach: As demonstrated by Apple and Amazon, success is largely dependent on innovation, continual improvement based on feedback, and exceptional customer service.

Innovation and Adaptability: As Tesla and Netflix have shown, remaining on the cutting edge of technology and remaining flexible in the face of change is what keeps legacy enterprises relevant.

Giving Back: Take inspiration from Patagonia and Bill Gates and participate in CSR projects and mentorship programs to positively impact society.

The Basis of a Legacy Enterprise

Vision and Purpose: The foundation of a legacy business is a compelling vision. Your goal should be more than just increasing profits; it should centre on the good that you wish to see happen in the world. What issue are you trying to solve? What kind of social influence are you hoping to have? Throughout the trip, your purpose will be your beacon of light.

Elon Musk, the creator of SpaceX and Tesla, is an example of a visionary company leader who highlights the importance of having a compelling vision. His goal of making the human race multiplanetary and implementing sustainable energy sources is an example of a purpose-driven strategy that has an impact that goes beyond business earnings.

Sustainable Growth: Older companies give priority to long-term development over short-term success. Put more effort into long-term plans that will safeguard the stability and health of your company rather than focusing on quick wins. This could entail reinvesting earnings, cultivating a devoted clientele, and consistently innovating.

A great illustration of sustainable expansion is Berkshire Hathaway, owned by Warren Buffett. Buffett has always focused on the inherent value of companies and maintained a long-term investment strategy, holding assets for many years. This tactic has produced significant wealth creation and left a legacy that will last for many decades.

Creating a Vibrant Corporate Culture: Legacy companies are known for having a strong corporate culture. Here's how to cultivate one: · basic principles: Determine and preserve basic principles that are consistent with your vision. The foundation of your corporate culture will be these ideals. Urge the members of your team to act with these principles in mind at all times.   For instance, Google's reputation as a global leader in technology has been shaped by its dedication to innovation, openness, and a collaborative work environment. The company's success has been fueled by these basic values, which have drawn top talent. · Employee Development: Make investments in the professional development of your staff members. Provide employees the chance to grow their skills, receive mentoring, and advance within the organisation. Long-term success requires a workforce that is both highly competent and motivated.

Adopting diversity and inclusion practices inside your organisation is crucial. A diverse workforce encourages creativity and makes sure your company stays relevant in a world that is changing by bringing a range of viewpoints and ideas to the table.

A Customer-First Mentality: A legacy company recognizes the value of its clientele. How to make them essential to your success is as follows:

· Outstanding Client Assistance Provide outstanding customer service on a regular basis. This entails paying close attention to detail, resolving problems quickly, and going above and above for clients.

Jeff Bezos's Amazon is well known for its customer-first philosophy. Amazon's reputation as a retail behemoth and a business with a long history has been cemented by its unwavering focus on customer satisfaction, which is demonstrated by its user reviews and quick delivery services.

Constant Improvement: Ask for and act upon client input to make improvements to your offerings. Demonstrate to your clients that you value their feedback and are dedicated to attending to their needs.

Steve Jobs's Apple is a shining example of a business that placed a high value on ongoing development in response to input from customers. Apple's continuous success and legacy may be attributed in large part to their iterative approach to product development, as is shown in the development of the iPhone.

Creativity and Flexibility: The essence of a legacy business is innovation. Embrace change to remain relevant:

Take Advantage of Technology: Keep abreast on technological developments in your field. Add fresh resources and methods to improve your goods and services.

Elon Musk's Tesla company exhibits a dedication to technological innovation in the automobile sector. By emphasising electric cars and autonomous driving technologies, the business positions itself as a leader in environmentally friendly mobility and lays the groundwork for a long-lasting legacy.

Remain flexible and adaptable when confronted with obstacles. Because the market is dynamic, being flexible lets you make adjustments as needed without sacrificing your long-term objectives.

Reed Hastings guided Netflix's transformation from a DVD rental firm to a massive streaming behemoth. Netflix's reputation in the entertainment sector has been cemented by its flexibility and readiness to accept new technology and changes in the market.

Contributing to the Community Legacy companies recognize the value of contributing to the community. Here's how you can influence things in a good way:

Participate in worthwhile corporate social responsibility (CSR) projects. Show that you are committed to improving the planet by helping out local charities and encouraging sustainability.

Under Yvon Chouinard's leadership, Patagonia is renowned for its steadfast dedication to environmental sustainability. The business demonstrates its commitment to protecting the environment for future generations through its CSR initiatives, such as the "1% for the Planet" campaign.

Mentoring and Education: Assist budding businesses by imparting your wisdom and expertise.

Co-founder of Microsoft Bill Gates has committed a sizable amount of his fortune to charitable endeavours via the Bill & Melinda Gates Foundation. The foundation has a significant beneficial legacy and focuses on global health, education, and poverty alleviation.

Creating a Positive Impact on Your Community: Contributing to Social and Economic Development

Entrepreneurship plays a significant role in both social and economic development. Ultimately, entrepreneurs have an impact on the economy through fostering innovation, generating new markets for goods and services, and building enterprises in addition to increasing their own wealth. You may read a comprehensive summary of the contribution of entrepreneurship to the social and economic advancement of a nation in this article.

The commitment of business venture to monetary and social turn of events

There are nine key conclusions about the role of entrepreneurship in social and economic development:

1. Increases Living Standards

The ability of entrepreneurship to significantly raise the standard of life for people and communities through the establishment of industries, the creation of wealth, and the creation of new jobs is a crucial role in economic development. In addition to creating jobs and sources of revenue on a broad scale, entrepreneurship has the ability to enhance people's quality of life by creating goods and services that are reasonably priced, secure, and bring value to their lives. Additionally, entrepreneurship creates new goods and services that eliminate the scarcity of necessities.

2. Financial Self-Sufficiency

Both the nation and the entrepreneur may be able to achieve financial independence through entrepreneurship. It encourages self-sufficiency and lessens the dependency of the country on imported goods and services. Exporting the produced goods and services to overseas markets can result in growth, independence, revenue inflow, and economic independence. Entrepreneurs also have total control over their financial destiny. They earn money and build wealth via their diligence and creativity, which enables them to attain financial security and economic independence.

3. Advantages of New Companies and Enterprises

To send off their firm, business visionaries decide the requests of the market and make arrangements with their labour and products. Business visionaries essentially affect the economy by sending off new organisations and undertakings, bringing about a more dynamic and different business climate. In addition to encouraging innovation and competition, entrepreneurship also results in the production of new and improved goods and services that support economic expansion.

4. Employment Generation

One significant calculation of the age of occupations is business. There are new job opportunities created by managing the operations of new enterprises and satisfying consumer expectations. In addition to fostering innovation and competition, entrepreneurship also stimulates investments and other entrepreneurs, resulting in the creation of new jobs across a variety of industries, including the manufacturing, construction, service, and technology sectors.

341

5. Promotes the Formation of Capital

The demonstration of social affair assets — like ventures and investment funds — to back new organisation attempts and advance monetary extension is known as capital creation. By luring investment, entrepreneurship can promote capital formation. A more varied and dynamic economy that promotes capital formation and opens the door to a variety of investment opportunities can also be developed through the founding of new companies and the expansion of already-existing ones.

6. Getting Rid of Poverty

Entrepreneurship has the capacity to alleviate poverty by creating jobs and promoting economic growth. Also, business supports the overall way of life and assists nearby economies with developing.

7. Community Advancement

Entrepreneurship raises the general standard of living, facilitates access to goods and services, and fosters economic progress. By providing services to underprivileged areas and creating environmentally friendly products, many entrepreneurs also positively impact their communities and enhance their well-being. Their efforts can support social and economic growth and help communities become stronger and more vibrant.

8. Most Effective Utilisation of Resources

Finding market possibilities and allocating resources as efficiently as feasible are two things that entrepreneurship may assist with. Furthermore, business visionaries are fundamental in making state of the art labour and products that fulfil customers' needs while utilising the current assets.

9. Increases per capita income and the gross national product

By raising the Gross Public Item (GNP) and Per Capita Pay (PCI), business can altogether add to monetary development and success. PCI decides the typical pay per individual, while GNP surveys a country's generally financial creation. PCI might ascend because of an expansion in GNP. By spawning new companies and sectors, entrepreneurship can boost the gross national product (GNP) and generate jobs, higher consumer spending, and more tax income.

Inspiring and Empowering Others: Sharing Your Entrepreneurial Journey and Encouraging Future Leaders

In addition to their inventions and enterprises, entrepreneurs are vital to the future because of their capacity to uplift and empower others. Entrepreneurs have the power to inspire and encourage future leaders to follow their passions and change the world by sharing their personal stories of entrepreneurship.

1. Tell Your Story Authentically

Be honest about your experiences as an entrepreneur, including the difficulties, disappointments, and victories. Genuineness establishes a connection with people and encourages them to think that they can accomplish their own objectives.

2. Emphasise the Value of Enthusiasm and Resilience

Stress the value of tenacity and passion when pursuing business endeavours. Tell about how your enthusiasm drove you and how your tenacity helped you overcome challenges.

3. Explain the Significance of Ongoing Education

Insist on the value of ongoing education and development. Tell about your experiences embracing innovation, learning new skills, and adjusting to shifting market conditions.

4. Stress the Importance of Growth and Failure

Normalise the idea that failing may be a teaching tool. Tell about the ways in which your mistakes taught you important lessons and advanced your career and personal development.

5. Highlight the Value of Cooperation and Teamwork

Accentuate how critical participation and collaboration are to progress. Give instances of how you and others have worked together to overcome obstacles and accomplish common objectives.

6. Promote Initiative and Risk-Taking

Encourage others to take initiative and welcome taking risks. Describe how taking measured chances and venturing outside comfort zones can result in opportunities and breakthroughs.

7. Offer guidance and mentoring

Aspiring entrepreneurs should receive mentoring and advice from you. To aid in their development, impart your wisdom, thoughts, and experience.

8. Acknowledge and Honour Successes

Celebrate and give thanks for other people's accomplishments, no matter how modest. An atmosphere of encouragement and support is fostered via positive reinforcement.

9. Establish Channels of Communication and Exchange

To help entrepreneurs and potential leaders interact, host workshops, seminars, or networking events.

10. Encourage Resources and Education for Entrepreneurship

Promote resource access and entrepreneurship education. Urge educational establishments to include entrepreneurship in their curricula and to offer programs of assistance to those who wish to become entrepreneurs.

Through their entrepreneurial experiences and the inspiration they provide, entrepreneurs can significantly contribute to the development of an innovative, creative, and constructive future. Their experiences can act as rays of hope and inspiration, inspiring the next generation of leaders to follow their passions and leave a lasting impression on the world.

Building a Sustainable and Thriving Business: Creating a Legacy of Innovation and Impact

Building a strong and sustainable business is about more than simply making money; it's about leaving a legacy of innovation and influence that goes beyond the balance sheet. It all comes down to building a company that endures, changes the world for the better, and motivates people to follow in your footsteps.

1. Welcome innovation and ongoing development

Innovation is essential in the fast-paced corporate environment of today. It is not a luxury. Always look for ways to make your processes, goods, and services better. Accept new techniques and embrace technology to improve the productivity and competitiveness of your company.

2. Give environmental responsibility and sustainability top priority.

Manage your company to reduce its adverse effects on the environment. Reduce your carbon footprint, adopt sustainable methods, and purchase goods ethically. Incorporate sustainability into your business plan and show that you are concerned about protecting the environment.

3. Encourage a Social Responsibility Culture

Integrate social responsibility into the operations and culture of your business. Encourage moral business conduct, participate in charitable endeavours, and assist neighbourhood communities. Show that you are dedicated to improving society in addition to your financial success.

4. Give Your Staff More Power and Encourage a Growth Mentality

Establish an atmosphere at work where staff members are empowered, appreciated, and encouraged to share their thoughts. Make investments in their education and training, offer them chances to advance, and foster an environment that values creativity and ongoing learning.

5. Establish Trusting Bonds with Partners and Customers

Put the needs of your customers first and cultivate a solid rapport with your suppliers and partners. In order to surpass customers' expectations, pay attention to their feedback, swiftly resolve any complaints they may have. Work together with partners to accomplish shared objectives and build relationships that will benefit both parties.

6. Continue to have a strategic direction and clear vision.

Clearly define the future you see for your business and set a strategic course that is consistent with your objectives and core values. Review your plan on a regular basis, adjust to shifting market conditions, and make wise choices that will help you remain sustainable over the long run.

7. Evaluate and Assess Your Work

Use important metrics to monitor your company's performance and conduct regular analysis of your findings. To maximise your operations, pinpoint areas that need work, compare your performance to industry norms, and make data-driven choices.

8. Adopt a resilient and adaptable mindset

Be ready to adjust to unanticipated obstacles, evolving technology, and shifting market conditions. Create a backup plan, foster a resilient culture inside your organisation, and show that you can overcome adversity and come out stronger.

9. Teach Others and Spread Your Knowledge

Talk to others about your business insights, encounters, and takeaways. Aspiring entrepreneurs might benefit from mentoring, attending industry events, and giving back to the larger business community. Encourage people to pursue their entrepreneurial aspirations and leave a beneficial legacy.

10. Leave an Innovative and Impactful Legacy

Make it your mission to create a company that improves the world while simultaneously making a profit. Not only should financial achievement be used to determine your legacy, but also the good that you have done in the world and the inspiration you have given to others.

Recall that creating a profitable and sustainable firm is a process rather than a final goal. It demands commitment to ongoing progress, tenacity, and determination. You may leave an innovative and significant legacy by embracing innovation, emphasising sustainability, empowering your team, and sharing your knowledge.

CONCLUSION

All in all, the excursion of beginning a private venture isn't without its difficulties, however it is likewise loaded up with huge open doors for development and achievement. By heeding the direction given in this article, hopeful business people can expand their possibilities exploring the cutthroat scene and building a flourishing business.

Keep in mind, the main characteristics for progress are enthusiasm, tirelessness, and versatility. In the event that you want to transform your thought into a reality, combined with the eagerness to learn and adjust en route, you can possibly accomplish extraordinary things.

As you leave on this pioneering experience, embrace the difficulties, commend the achievements, and never neglect to focus on your vision. The world requires your interesting thoughts and the energy to rejuvenate them. With devotion and assurance, you can turn out to be important for the developing pool of effective business visionaries moulding the eventual fate of business.

Embrace the excursion, gain from your encounters, and never abandon your fantasies. The world is sitting tight for your inventive thoughts and the effect you can make. Go forward, gallant business visionary, and let your business sprout!

Review page

Dear Reader,

I hope this finds you well.

I'm contacting you today since I esteem your perspective and would be unbelievably thankful if you would save a chance to drop a review. I've been dealing with this undertaking for a long while, and your feedback would be important to me

In particular, I'm keen on your viewpoints on the accompanying perspectives:

Clearness: Is the substance simple to follow and get it? Are there any parts that could be made more clear or more succinct?

Commitment: Does the substance keep you intrigued all through? Does it actually pass on the expected message and inspire the ideal feelings?

Handiness: Does the substance give important bits of knowledge and data? Does it address the requirements and interests of its ideal interest group?

Generally Impression: What is your general impression of the substance or item? What sticks out, and what regions could be refined?

I'm sure that your legit and productive criticism will have a massive effect in the nature of this undertaking. Your experiences are really valued.

Thank you for contemplating my request. I can hardly hold on to hear your thoughts.

Best respects,

Kate W. Cavill

www.ingramcontent.com/pod-product-compliance
Lightning Source LLC
Chambersburg PA
CBHW072134290526
45794CB00004B/1317